Order in the House

Who's Leading You

FELICE

ORDER IN THE HOUSE:

Copyright@2017by **Felicia Cauley (Felice)**

All rights reserved. No part of this publication may be reproduced, distributed or transmitted in any form or by any means, without prior written permission.

Right Side Publishing
P.O Box 339
Reynoldsburg, Ohio
www.rightsidepublishing.com

Scripture Quotations are taken from the Holy Bible, King James version Copy right KJV latest verslon, New International, NIV latest version, English Standard version ESV version. Places and incidents are a product of the author's life experiences. Locales and public names are sometimes used for atmospheric purposes. Non-fiction names have been changed actual people, living or dead, or to businesses, companies, events, institutions, or locales is completely coincidental.

Book cover Design by Tiny Communications
Author Photo by Tiny Communications
Editor Elizabeth Morris

Order In The House
Who's Leading You

FELICE

ORDER IN THE HOUSE:

DEDICATION

Married couples that I know who are examples
of what a Godly family should look like:

My Pastor Dr. Lafayette(Theresa) Scales from
Rhema Christian Center

My Uncle and Aunt,
Bishop John C. Pace and Mary Pace

Pastor Dan and Margret Harris

My Sister and Brother
Ebonie(John) Banks

My cousins
Latonya (Wade)Crumwell
Pastor William (Lajuana)Taylor
Monica (Terrell) Guidry
Eric (Lauren) Tillman Jr
Gregory(Debbie) Harris
Michael(Tori)Alston

Friends and Leaders of Kingdom Prosperity Ministries

Samuel and Rotausha Caliman

CONTENTS

Acknowledgements 7

Forward 9

1. **Our Place In The Home** 17
2. **What Happen When Our House Is Out Of Order?** 49
3. **Handling Our Finances** 57
4. **How We Treat Each Other** 73
5. **When Do We Say We're Sorry** 100
6. **Restoring Our Broken Families** 105
7. **A Family Designed By God** 118
8. **Love Is A Choice** 128
9. **Forgiveness** 136
10. **Trust** 149
11. **Respect** 161

12. Invaders	**168**
13. Deliverance	**180**
14. Will God Bless A Family That Doesn't Acknowledge Him?	**190**
15. Faith	**197**
16. God Calls Us To Have Order	**228**
17. Cleansing	**234**
18. A House of Peace	**244**
19. No More Shame	**252**
20. Honoring Our Family Members	**256**
21. Sticking It Out	**262**
22. Use Your Resources	**272**
23. Prayer	**274**
Notes/Journal	**278**

ACKNOWLEDGEMENTS

Jesus Christ is my Lord and Savior. Through Him, all things are possible! Special thanks to my husband, Robert Cauley, for having patience with me through the publishing process of this book and for always making sure that I had the technology I needed to complete Order in the House and every book that I have worked on before this one. You are indeed my rock. I love you! Thanks to my children Micleicia, John, Johnesha, and Antalicia who allowed me to share some of their life stories with the world. I would like to thank my cousins, Eric Tillman Jr. and friend Theresa Scott, for sharing my books with their clients. Also, Danshell Taylor, you encouraged me with little words that meant so much. You knew just what to have me read to keep me going when I wanted to give up. Special thanks to Pastor Donald J Washington and Lady Shirley Washington our spiritual mom and dad. Robert and I will never be able to thank you enough for your marital council and advice.

ORDER IN THE HOUSE:

Forward

Order in the House: Who's Leading You?

In society today, people tend to do what they want to do in their households instead of what is right. Have you ever heard of these phrases before?

"I pay the cost to be the boss."

"I can do what I want to do in my own house; I pay the bills here."

The question is who determines what is the right way to run our homes? Is it men, women, God, or the government?

Women have begun to lead the household. Years ago, men used to work, and women stayed home with the children. Today, both men and women must work. Women are now earning their own money and have been for a while. They are strong leaders in the work place. Some women even own their own companies. They are the C.E.O.'s over their businesses, but are they the leaders in their homes?

ORDER IN THE HOUSE:

Times have changed. I believe women have always worked outside of the home in each generation, just not as much as the women do today. Women of days past understood how important it was to be home with their children. In today's world, many children come home from school; with no parents present. In most homes, this is not by choice; but due to single-parent households or income. Some people just can't make ends meet on one income. Since people seem to feel that their children can be responsible at different ages, the government has decided what age a child can stay home alone and how late a teenager can stay out at night.

The Word of God shows us the order for our household by scripture example and what happens when our household is out of order. People may never agree on how the household should be lead; but most people will agree that when things get out of order, it's a mess. When there is a mess, someone must clean it up! Sometimes, it takes a long time to clean up a mess. It might take more than one person to get things in order. One person must be willing to help. The other person must be willing to lead. It's better to find out what order the house should be ran in before it becomes a mess.

In almost every organization, there are leaders. At church, you have God, the Pastor, Elders, Ministers, and the list goes on. In the work place, there are Managers, Supervisors, and Team Leaders. It may differ from job to job. However, there is always an authority figure to keep things in order, so why not have leaders in the home?

In a single-parent household, it is hard at times to determine who the leader in the home is. With older children in the home, it's even more difficult, especially when boys think that they are men. They will often say, "I got this" to mom or dad. Some parents teach their boys that they must be the man of the house when the father is absent. What a responsibility for a boy to have! Boys are strong and tough. They can deal with a lot. We mean well as parents, but sometimes we put our children in roles that they can't handle.

Girls, on the other hand, can be a handful. They think that they have all the answers, especially when they are the oldest child in the home. Most of them take the lead in the home and tell their siblings what to do and how to do it. I know this all too well, because I'm the oldest of my siblings. My oldest daughter will take the lead automatically without thinking about it.

In a single-parent household where mom or dad must work, the older children will sometimes be in charge of the younger children, making them leaders. There are three states currently in the United States that have laws to determine what age parents can leave their children alone legally. Illinois requires children to be 14-years of age before they can be home alone; in Maryland, the minimum age is 8-years; while in Oregon, children must be 10-years before being home alone. This is just an example to show you how the government has allowed states to choose their own laws when it comes to our families. I find it interesting that right now, only three states have these laws. Laws will change from time to time, which can make it hard to know what to do or how to raise our children.

I know I must follow the law, but I live in Ohio. There are no laws on what age we Ohioans can leave our children home alone. For me, 8-years-old is too young. Thank God, this book is about family and not what is the appropriate age to leave children at home. Is there an order the single family should follow? Who decides that order? Is it the adult in the home, the government, or God?

Whenever I have a problem that I can't fix, I pray to God and then ask my husband for advice. Sometimes, I go straight to my husband because I believe that he is a man of God. When he doesn't have the answer, he will pray to God; and then get back with me when he has the answer. Other times, we will pray together. My husband follows God, and I follow him. Our children obey us, understanding that my husband has the last say in our home. We have certain things that we are in-charge of.

I have been around different couples, and they all operate differently when it comes to finances, children, and household chores. In a single-parent household, one person handles everything. When it comes to God, the order for the single-parent household doesn't differ from a two-parent household in a marriage between a man and woman.

I don't know if the government really cares about who's leading the home. Parents are to provide for their children until the age of eighteen, unless they are in college. Governments help to create laws. People should govern their own households. When they don't, the law will be enforced. When men and women fight in the home, someone may go to jail.

When we follow the laws of God, we shouldn't have to worry about going to jail. God's laws do set order in the home. However, God doesn't have a rule or law that parents must follow when it comes to what age a child should be left at home alone. That calls for good, old common sense. We were born with a measure of faith. I'm not sure if we all have common sense. That's another book in itself!

Order in the House: Who's Leading You? will help you look at your home. Examine the order of your house and who's leading you. I'm not an expert when it comes to the order in the home. I do believe God's way is best. We learn His ways through the Bible. When God gave me the title for this book, I said, "Hmm." As I began to ask the Lord what the book was about, He began to show me life when I was single and now that I'm married. I prayed and said, "Lord, use me however you see fit;" so, here we are.

I'm sharing real life experiences with you. I had to do a lot of studying and seeking God, because this wasn't an easy book to write. I often say that my life is not my own. I'm an open book before the

Lord. Why He chose me to write this book, I don't know. It might just be because I'm a willing vessel to share some uncomfortable things in my life to help others. I am giving God all the honor and glory for all families whose lives will be changed by this book. I encourage you to share this book with your loved ones, and I hope you enjoy it.

CHAPTER 1
OUR PLACE IN THE HOME

Do we have the same roles, Men women, husband and wives; where do the children fit in? In this chapter; we will learn our positions in the home as husband and wife, our children's roles, and what the positions of a single-parent household are. I believe that God's love for men, women, and children are the same. He has given us various positions and roles for a reason. God should be the C.E.O. of our homes. The C.E.O. is the highest person in a company and responsible for important decisions.

ORDER IN THE HOUSE:

C.E.O. stands for chief executive officer. God is our maker; He is our chief executive officer. When we allow Him to rule our lives and have full reign in our households, he sets the order in the home. He is our leader. We are positioned by Him. He has placed the husband as the head of the house. The wife is to be his helpmate. The world has their standards in the workplace. In an office setting, there's usually an office manager. The manager runs the office. When there is a problem the employees can't handle, they go to the manager. Who makes the final decision? Anything that the manager can't handle he meets with the C.E.O to get instructions. The manager then goes and instructs the employees. It is very rare that anyone outside of the company management speaks to the Chief Executives Officer. Thank God, it's not like that with God. He is the C.E.O over our homes. The husband is the head. Yes, the wife is his helpmate. The difference is that they both have access to God. Neither of them need to make an appointment. I always tell my husband if he gets out of line that I'm going straight to the pastor who married us. Really, I will go to the throne of God first. I will say, "God, this is the man that I married in Your presence. Lord, he is out of order. Please help him get it together." There's never been a time that the Lord has given me a word for my husband to tell him how to lead. He has revealed to me what I should do to make things better for my husband. A lot of the time, it is knowing when to speak and when to be quiet, which is easier said than done. My husband seems to be good at being slow to speak. Sometimes I may ask him a question, and he's quiet. I'll say, "Sweet, do you hear me?"

"Yes, babe", he'll answer.

I'll look at him; he'll look at me. Then I'll say, "Okay, pray about it!"

That's one good thing about a house ran by God. We know each other's boss. I can now say that we are on different levels. I'm glad we are too, just like in the Garden of Eden,

ORDER IN THE HOUSE:

God gave Adam and Eve instructions not to eat of the fruit from the tree of knowledge of good and evil. When they disobeyed God, God questioned Adam first. He could have asked both of them. Read the book of Genesis, the first book of the Bible. In this book, God establishes the order for the family. We also can see what happens when we don't obey the order that God has for us. Because of the book of Genesis, I have a great deal of respect for my husband's role as the head of our household. I have no desire to have his role. I pray for him every day because I understand that he is accountable to God.

He has to answer to Him on how our house is ran; so, if you really look at God's order for the home, there is no question who should be leading us. God is the C.E.O., is He leading you?

When I look at things that way, I get a clear picture of His plan for me as a wife. He loves me so much that He has given me a husband under His authority -- not to rule me in an unpleasant way, but to protect me and shield me from the hands of the enemy. He has given me a husband to comfort, love, and pray for me. He's to provide for me. Knowing all that, I am honored to walk beside my husband. I have no problem following him as long as he follows Christ. I even find myself asking him what we should do, trying to stay in tune with my husband.

I remember my aunt told me a story once about her and my uncle (who is a Pastor). They were in a store, and it was being robbed. My aunt was further down the aisle and away from my uncle, who was shopping. My uncle looked up and saw two men coming into the store holding up guns. He walked over to my aunt and said, "Give me your purse".

She handed it to him. He grabbed it and hid it underneath some beams in the store. Then he whispered to my aunt, "The store is being robbed".

When he peeked down the aisle, he could see the men waving their guns at the cashiers. They didn't even know that my aunt and uncle were in the store. My uncle looked at my aunt and said to her,

"Let's go to the back of the store". They got to the back of the store and saw a door; they opened the door and ran for their lives. That happened about thirteen years ago. I don't know if my uncle had time to even pray. I believe they prayed as they ran.

My aunt listened to my uncle (her husband). If she would have questioned him as to why he needed her purse, they may not have lived to see today. Thank God that I am a wife! I know my aunt had to have total trust in my uncle to hand him her purse. I might have said, "What! Give you my purse?"

Pow! Boom! I would have gotten my husband and I killed. There are many nuggets of wisdom in that story. In order for my aunt to give my uncle her purse; not only did she trust in him, but she also submitted to him. Women and men, we must change our mindset! She submitted. He didn't control her. He could have snatched her purse and thrown her down. He knew his wife. It wouldn't have been bad if he did push her down to the floor to save her life, but he chose not to.

I know that in the world today, all men are not Godly men. They don't follow the order of God. Some men and women don't believe in the Word of God. There should be an order in the house, and we all should know who's leading our home and what our roles are in the home.

Later, we will explore what happens when our home is out of order. I'm learning everyday how to be a wife. God prepared me long before I got married. Before I got married, I was a single mom with four children. Many times, I thought that I was alone. I always prayed to God for direction and instructions on raising my children. I made mistakes, as parents do. I realized that no parent is perfect. I learned long ago how important it was to have rules and guidelines in the home to create order.

Sometimes I became mixed up when it came to who was leading the household. After all, I was single. No one could tell me what to do, at least no man, and not in my house. My house? Where I paid the bills? I was indeed the C.E.O. I knew that God gave me my children; and I was to nourish them, protect them, provide for them, and teach them the ways of the Lord. I must say; I found out early on that I was not the chief executive officer in my home. Can you believe that? Not even when I was a single mother! It was then that I found out what the saying "Being married to God" meant. With four children, I was always in the presence of the Lord asking for help even when I was out of the will of God.

    Single men or women, it doesn't matter. God should be leading your home. God wants to be the leader of all our homes according to His Word. As a single mother, I sought God for direction. This made me humble towards the Lord and has helped me a great deal in my marriage. I realized that even before I got married, I was not the leader in my home. I leaned and depended on God. Now I lean and depend on my God and husband. We are not on the same level. The husband is positioned by God to be the head of the house, and the wife is his helpmate.

The wife can't be the head and a helpmate. She can head various aspects of the home, but she is not to be in charge of leading the home. The husband takes on that responsibility. There's a reason for this. The husband is to bare his wife's burdens. The Bible states that women are the weaker vessels. I never thought I would be happy to be called the weaker vessel. When I think about how Christ bore our burdens on the cross, I get excited. Christ told husbands to love their wives as Christ has loved the church and gave Himself up for her

(Ephesians 5:25). Christ went through a lot of pressure on the cross. Men in general can handle a great deal of pressure. I know my husband can. He will go to work, put everything on the back burner, and just focus on work. I, on the other hand, will go to work and be thinking about what's going on at home, bills, and many other things at once. If things are out of order at home, there's no way I can focus at work. I am more emotional than my husband. We are built different, so we handle things differently.

When women are dealing with too much pressure, it will show in some way.

When I was a single parent, I dealt with a lot of pressure by myself. I was the one who made decisions and had to fix everything. Before I got married, I consulted God when I made decisions. He just couldn't get my attention because I was in an unhealthy relationship, but that's another book. I know people could visually see that I was dealing with a lot of pressure. I have eczema, it showed on my face with my skin-It would flair up by my nose. I would pick at the dry skin until it became dark. When we take on more than we can handle, it can show physically. I haven't had that problem now that I have the position as a helpmate.

God wants husbands to cherish their wives. This doesn't mean that women are physically weaker than men. Some women are physically stronger than men. No matter how strong a woman is, she should have a need for her husband. She should be able to lean and depend on him. There's an old church song that goes like this, "Leaning, leaning, I'm safe and secure from all harm. Leaning on Christ my Savior. Leaning on the Everlasting Arm".

This song tells us to trust and depend on the Lord. The Lord is our leader. The husband must depend on God. He is the head of the house, but he is to be humble before the Lord. The Bible says that the
wife is the weaker vessel. Therefore, the husband must be weak himself when it comes to God. He must realize that he must lean and depend on God for all his family's needs. Sure, he may go out, get a job, and provide for his family, but God will lead him to the job!

"Trust in the LORD with all thine heart; and lean not unto thine own understanding. In all thy ways acknowledge Him, and He shall direct thy paths" (Proverbs chapter 3:5-6,).

We have various positions in Christ and in the church, as well as in our homes; but God loves us the same. In the church, we have pastors, elders, deacons, and teachers. There are many positions. Each one has a job.

The pastor may have a higher position than the deacon may. The deacon's job is still just as important. The pastor needs the deacon, and the deacon has a need for the pastor. The pastor feeds the sheep, and the deacon cares for them and nurtures them. That's just a small example of their job description. In the home, the husband is the provider and protector. He also nourishes, but he is commanded by God to provide for his family (Genesis 3:17). God provided everything Adam and Eve needed in the garden.

When Adam followed his wife, he was punished and told to work for his food. This is the beginning of a family out of order. We'll talk about that later. In the garden, Adam and Eve both trust God to take care of all their needs. Adam had a need for God. God loved him so much that He gave him a help mate. He didn't want Adam to be alone.

As a married woman, I know what my position in the home is as a help mate. I used to wonder what all that entailed. Would it be helping my husband spiritually? Yes, I will help him in ministry. I just can't tell him what to do in ministry. When it comes to helping my husband spiritually, I had to learn how to keep my mouth shut. When we first got married, I could hear the spirit of God saying, "SHUT UP! SHUT UP! You don't have all the answers". I found myself watching to see if my husband read his Bible. One day my husband and I were discussing the Bible when he shared with me that he reads his Bible every morning before work. I thought, "Wow, I didn't have to tell him to read his Bible every day". It may sound funny, but sometimes we as women seem to think that we are supposed to lead our husbands spiritually. What a responsibility to have! I'll take being his help mate. We are to not only help him with his spiritual needs through prayer and fasting. We are to not only help with our husbands spiritual needs through prayer and fasting; we are his help mate in everything, every area where he needs help. There have been times that my husband has come to me for advice. Sometimes I give him advice.

Other times I direct him to the elders of the church or his mentor.

When God reveals to me my husband's gifts and shows me where he's taking my husband, I get real excited. I love my husband and want the best for him always. I realize that it's not my job to get him where he's going. There are times that my husband doesn't even see himself where God has revealed to me he will be. When we first got married, God would show me things about our marriage. No sooner than when he would show me, I would wave a flag in my husband's face. "Babe," I would say, "Listen, the Lord showed me that you have the gift of healing. "Oh, and He's going to use us together in ministry.

"Babe, babe, do you hear me?" My husband would just look at me. "Um hum", he'd say, "Ok". No matter how many flags I wave in his face, he should get a revelation from God. I'm learning more and more when to speak and when not to speak. I'm practicing praying and listening. I also enjoy hearing the stories that my husband shares with me. He has ministered to different couples. That is the vision that the Lord showed me when we first got married!

My husband and I were best friends before we got married. We shared a lot with each other, so it was only natural to think that I should share every vision that the Lord showed me with him. Part of trusting in our Savior is believing that He has a plan for our husbands. He will lead and guide them into all truth. We have the same Holy Spirit. God's in control, not me. I must say, I do feel good when my husband asks for my opinion, realizing that I'm his help mate. We have a need for each other; the need for each other and the need for God to keep us humble towards God and each other. Although we are on various levels and have different positions, we can share each other's visions and help each other fulfill God's plan for our lives.

I'm his helpmate, but he also helps me. How awesome! God's way is the best, not society or our own. Society seems to think that women should do for men by cooking, cleaning and being sex objects. What about women's live? No need for men. We can do it all ourselves.

I'd rather follow the Bible way. The Bible tells us we are to treat each other with lowliness, meekness, and long suffering, forbearing one another in love (Ephesians 4:2). We understand that we need God and each other. I enjoy when my husband cooks breakfast for me. If we followed society, he certainly wouldn't be cooking breakfast for me. I believe this is a display of lowliness and meekness put together. Helping each other with chores are not hard; helping one another achieve our spiritual goals is a different story. I have a desire to go into the mission field, travel all over the world and offer hope to the lost through Jesus Christ. That's not my husband's desire.

I can remember discussing missions with him. One day, our church had "Missions Sunday". That's when we get reports on how our mission teams are doing. There was a couple who moved their whole family to China for the ministry. They told us how God was working in China. As the husband and wife gave their testimonies, tears came to my eyes. My heart was beating so fast. I turned and looked at my husband and I said, "Missions! Missions! Yes! I've wanted to do this for a while!" As I was explaining to my husband how bad I wanted to go, I could hear the man saying, "Don't worry about the money to go. God will make a way for you".

"Yes! Yes!" I screamed loud in my mind.

Then before I knew it, I jumped up out of my seat and yelled, "Hallelujah!" My husband sat in his seat.

When we got home, we discussed it more. He said, "I'm not going. You can go on your own". I laughed. I know that if God wants me to go into the mission's ministry, He will make away. The Lord can use me in missions and my husband somewhere else, but we must be on the same page. He'll use us together in everything. He may have different plans for us in the ministry itself, but He never sends us in different directions.

We don't always have the same visions. Sometimes we have to pray long and hard to get what the other's vision is. Once we can picture the vision, we grab a hold of the vision, and watch God work. My husband may never go into the mission's ministry. He may never physically go minister in another country. We are one body. Where I am, He is also. When it's time for me to go, he will cover me in prayer. God's timing is the best. I won't go anywhere unless it's time. I'm a strong woman. I need God and man. No women's live! I need my husband. Thank God, I'm not by myself.

For anyone who's single, you're not alone. God is your husband. That's what it means to be married to God. While you're single, that is. If you desire a mate, He will give you a mate. I believe that is a book in itself.

Just knowing that God gives us different dreams and visions and that He has planned our life according to our destiny is awesome. Oh, how wonderful it is when He gives us the same visions. It doesn't matter if we have different goals as long as we fulfill God's ultimate goal for our life. That is to live in unity with each other and Him- **One body in Christ**. I know that I'm not on the same level with God as my husband is. We have various positions, not only am I his help mate, the Bible says that I am the keeper of the home. I know most women are clean and can keep up a good house, but when I read this in the Bible, I thought to myself, "What else does this mean?" He gave me the answer in Proverbs, the thirty-first chapter. You must read the book of Proverbs. Every time I read this chapter, I get more and more insight on what God expects from me as a wife.

This book of the Bible speaks of a virtuous woman. Proverbs gives detail of what a virtuous woman should be like. It refers to her as a keeper of the home. There's no doubt in my mind that that woman was a clean woman. I also get a picture in my mind that she was a peaceful woman. She prepared for her husband to arrive home from work. She made sure the children were taken care of. In this day and time, that might mean helping with homework or making sure chores are done. I believe that she set the atmosphere for her husband to come home to a place of rest. In the world we live in today, both husbands and wives must work. It's not always easy for the wife to set the tone in the home before the husband gets home. Most of the time, I'm just as tired as my husband. Since I get home from work first, I try to relax. I also take care of my daughter and the dogs and maybe cook, which I don't get to do a lot of.

The world we live in today has changed so much. There's so much going on outside of our homes. Our homes should be like a sanctuary full of peace and rest. We should be able to renew our strength in our homes through prayer and worship, even in tough times, when both are working. It's not easy; there have been times when my husband and I have fallen victims to a routine. Our conversation becomes more like a dialogue. "Hi, babe!" I'd say.

"Hi", he would reply, "how was your day?"

I believe that the wife, as the keeper of the home, can also change the atmosphere. When I see my husband and I are following a routine and not communicating, I will do something unusually different. Instead of talking about our day, we'll talk about what day it is. I'll say, "Well, Babe, it's Tuesday. I think we can make it". Robert will look at me and laugh. Then he'll say, "Yes!". Then out of the blue, I'll say, "I'm glad you're my husband". Having a routine is good, but not if we continue in the same way each day on autopilot.

Not only do we do this in our homes but also at church. We go to church, stand up, clap our hands, listen to the word, and pay our tithes; but maybe not always in that order. Nothing's wrong with any of the above. It is when we are so used to a set order that we can't hear from God. In our homes, we can get so used to a habit that we are greeting each other and not really hearing one another. When I said to

Robert, "Well, Babe, it's Tuesday" instead of "Hi", I got his attention!

Anyone can keep a house clean. It takes a woman of God to be a true keeper of the home. Only the Word of God can show us how. There's a lot more to a virtuous woman. I can tell you that my husband and I had been married for five years when I first started writing this book. Now, we have been married for ten years.

I'm still focused on being a good keeper of the home. We have four children, one granddaughter, a grandson, and a grandson on the way. Our family is loud. We have actors, musicians, dancers, writers, artists, comedians, teachers, and preachers. We are a very talented family. On any given day, you may come to visit and find yourself at a concert or Bible study right in our home. You never know what to expect!

My husband is a man of little words. He loves his quiet time. The children love to entertain themselves, as well as others. If I don't set a cut off time; they will sing, dance, and tell jokes all night. Don't get me wrong, I love to entertain also. I also know how it feels to come home to a nice peaceful home, not so much the quietness but freedom from confusion. When my husband comes home, I'm excited to see him and can't wait to hear how his day went. I try not to start with "Guess what!" or "You won't believe this". That is not an effective way to start a conversation after a long day at work, but it also depends on how my day has gone.

Robert and I were best friends before we got married. There are days when I have started our conversation with "Guess what, babe!" There are other times where I must give him his space. I'm learning that men just need space sometimes. I try to let the children know that also. I think learning how to give our husbands space has got to be part of a virtuous woman's character. Thank God, we have different roles in the home. Giving him his own space creates a peaceful home.

ORDER IN THE HOUSE:

Even the world knows that sometimes men need their space. They call it a man cave. In the Christian home, I don't believe there should be a man cave. I don't want my husband to barricade himself in a room. I like to see him sometimes interact with the family. We don't have a den at our house now, but we do agree that the den belongs to him. Everything is ours, together. Peace in the home. The Bible says blessed are the peacemakers for they shall be called the children of God (Matthew 5:9).

As the keeper of the home, I realize it's much easier to keep a home clean. It takes a lot more than a mop and a broom to keep peace in the home. There are a lot of different forces that can destroy the peace in our home. It can be our family, children, and even our friends. Sometimes family can interrupt our schedule with their schedule. They mean well and may not know the routine in our home. Our children, who do know our schedule, can try to use it to their advantage. We cannot let our children manipulate us by playing us against each other. Our friends, we love them dearly; but they live at their house and we live at ours. The good thing is that we have surrounded ourselves around Godly people. They understand that God is the C.E.O. of our homes.

In this chapter, we have explored the role of men and women in the home as husband and wife with the understanding that in the single-family home, God is the C.E.O. in the home. God has created us so unique. He loves us so much that He gives us real clear instructions to follow in our homes. We have only touched the surface with the role of the husband and the wife as protector and keeper of the home. There's so much more that God has commanded us to do in our homes. It differs for men, women, and children. The children really have it good. They do have a role in the home. I tell our children all the time to study the Bible to see what their roles are and to study the promises of God for their lives. We, as parents, are accountable for how we raise our children. They, in turn, are commanded by God to love and obey us as their parents and to obey those who rule over them. Children are to honor their father and mother that their days may be long on the earth. They do have a very important role. One is to be *children while they're children, enjoying* their childhood and worrying about nothing. I know not all children have good homes. If you are a child reading his book; I have good news for you! The Bible says, "Suffer little children and forbid them not, to come unto me: For of such is the Kingdom of Heaven" (Matthew 19:14) KJV

God is still your C.E.O. Trust and follow Him through His Word.

I believe we make our parents proud as adults by raising our children by the guidelines that we have been taught through the Word of God, which can be passed down from generation to generation. The Bible doesn't teach us that we must do everything the way that our parents did. We just need to follow the principles that they have laid out before us. When I grew up, there was no foul language in our home. Even though my mother was a young mother who was raising me with the help of my grandmother in the seventies, she never cursed at me. I raised my children in an environment free of violence, foul language, and drugs. I must admit there have been times when our children have made us want to curse.

On the other hand, my husband came from a family who loves to curse. When we first got married, I can remember my husband saying a few choice words when he got mad. I'd say that's not Christian-like. He'd say, "I know; I need prayer". He is better now. If he were to even slip and say anything not of God, be it the S-word or any foul word at all; our youngest daughter will send conviction to his heart. When I was growing up, there were so many curse words that were foreign to our household, but not in my friends' households. These words were words like "darn", "what the heck", "snap", "shut up", "dang", "dag", "oh man", and "gosh". There are too many to name. "Shut up" is one of my favorite ones. We were never allowed to say the words "shut up". If any one of us kids used that word over at my grandmother's house, woo wee! She would make whoever said, "shut up" go outside and pick a switch off the tree. What would make it so bad was the child that the other child told to shut up, could help pick a switch. This would be the switch she would use to whip the misbehavior's behind. If the switch wasn't big enough, she'd make them get another one. My grandmother wasn't someone to play with. "MaDea", my cousin would call her, was no joke!

I must say, I'm still a work in progress. I wonder what my grandmother would say to me today if she heard me tell my youngest daughter to shut up. I don't know what she would say, but I do know that she wouldn't play with her nor toil with her as long as I have. Robert and I have agreed that my youngest daughter must be told to shut up sometimes. If not, she will plead her case until the sun either rises or goes down. Since we don't practice using a switch as my grandmother did, shut up will have to do, and maybe a couple of slaps.

Growing up with a mother and a grandmother who didn't use foul language has helped me become a woman who respect others. I try not to use my mouth to hurt or destroy others. I admit, growing up
 in a household without foul language has made me also look stupid when I have tried to express myself

using curse words in the past. By the time I had turned twenty, I established a good character for myself. Cursing just wasn't in my character. It just wasn't lady like to me. I learned to hold people accountable for their actions also. Therefore, I didn't allow cursing in my home.

Still today, I don't allow cursing in my home. My husband has one uncle who reminds me of Fred Sanford; he has a very filthy mouth. I think that children try to gather around just to hear what's going to come out of his mouth. Yet and still he tries hard to control his mouth when he's in our home. Thank God! My husband and I now have two grandchildren who are being raised free of foul language in the home. We have four generations. We are trying to hold to the principles of God. I know that would not only make my mother proud, but my grandmother proud also. We are good parents today because we are watching our children follow the principles of God.

The Bible also speaks about children growing up to be blessed in many ways. Here are a few scriptures:

"Praise the Lord! Blessed is the man who fears the Lord, who greatly delights in His commandments! His offspring will be mighty in the land; the generation of the upright will be blessed. Wealth and riches are in his house, and his righteousness endures forever. Light dawns in the darkness for the upright; he is gracious, merciful, and righteous. It is well with the man who deals generously and lends; who conducts his affairs with justice" (Psalm 112:1-10).

"I have no greater joy than to hear that my children are walking in the truth"

(3 John 1:4, ESV).

"Besides this, we have had earthly fathers who disciplined us and we respected them. Shall we not much more be subject to the Father of spirits and live? For they disciplined us for a short time as it seemed best to them, but he disciplines us for our good, that we may share his holiness. For the moment, all discipline seems painful rather than pleasant, but later it yields the peaceful fruit of righteousness to those who have been trained by it" (Hebrews 12:9-11, ESV).

God loves children and families who raise their children up to be righteous. They are blessed. Children are placed in a position to bring honor to the family. We must teach our children what their place is in the family, so that they are a blessing to us. We will receive blessings for generations to come.

I have seen these Biblical principles come alive in a family that I have known over the years. My pastor is a very blessed man. He has trained his children to honor and revere God. His mother is blessed. I believe she's in her 90's or close to it. Pastor's mother has been sick a few times, but God has honored his prayers. I know others have also prayed. God has truly been a promise keeper. Whenever our pastor gets blessed, he blesses his wife, children, and mother. He continues to be blessed; the more he's blessed the more he gives. My pastor set the tone when he taught his children the principles of God, and they are now practicing them with their children.

CHAPTER 2

WHAT HAPPENS WHEN OUR HOUSE IS OUT OF ORDER?

Our house becomes out of order when God is not the leader in our home. This happens when we think that we have all the answers and not God. We feel as if we don't have to seek instructions on raising our children, handling our finances, as well as dealing with one another. We may feel as if we have all the answers, or we feel like we have a right to do what we want in our own home.

The Bible instructs us on how to raise our children. If we follow His plan, we can't go wrong. Our children are going to make mistakes, we all do. Following the Word of God doesn't free us from challenges; it instructs us on how to make the right decisions. The Bible said if we train up our children the way that they should go; they shouldn't depart when they get old. That means when we put the Word in our children; when they are faced with adversity, that Word comes alive. The Word of God is their resource. It is up to us as parents to provide them with this resource. When they make wrong choices, we are to instruct them by the Word of God.

God had a set order in the Garden of Eden. Everything that Adam and Eve needed was right there in the garden. He gave them one command, not to eat of the fruit from the tree of good and evil. You know how the story goes. If not, you should read it in Genesis, at least the first three chapters. I believe that most parents want the best for their children just like God wanted for us. There are still consequences when we don't follow the order that God has for our homes.

One of them is fear of abuse. I've never seen so many parents afraid of their children. It's on the news all the time. Some parents have lost control of their children. The children seem to believe that they run the household. They don't fear God or their parents. There are young people who are selling drugs in the home, having sex, and refusing to go to school. Their actions have caused a serious affect in our communities. The crime rate is high all over, even in some suburban communities. They have no respect for themselves or their elders. I saw on the news that an elderly man about seventy-eighty years old got shot by a man in his twenties. The young man came busting in his house to rob and maybe even kill him. What a shame!

More and more young girls are getting pregnant in middle school and high school. The graduation rate of high school graduates has dropped in some communities. Secondary schools used to be for those students who were either misbehaving or pregnant. Now days it's to give students who drop out of school a second chance.

I grew up in the seventies and was raised by my grandmother, who was a God-fearing woman. In those days we didn't hear of many parents on the news saying, they didn't know what to do with their children. No fear, Parents would whip their children quick. Sometimes the neighbor would even help. No adult, anywhere whatsoever or at any time, allowed their child or anyone else's child to disrespect them. Now we live in the twenty-first century where no one wants anyone but themselves to tell their children what to do. Half of the time these parents aren't teaching their own children what's right and what's wrong. How can we expect to have the blessings of God flow through our household when we're not obeying God's laws for the home?

We must stand firm as parents, single parents as well as married. God's promises when it comes to our children are the same for married parents as well as single parents. This is good because I have been a single parent. It's not easy raising children single or married. The enemy will try using our children, even when we follow the laws of God.

God remains true to His promises. The Bible tells us as parents to train up our children by the principles of God's Word (Proverbs 22:6, KJV). In Proverbs, this is a promise to parents.

We should believe the Word of God; even when our children go astray, and they will. The Word says when they get old; they will not depart. In the story of the prodigal son, he asked his father to give him his inheritance while he was yet alive. Doesn't that remind you of some of our children today? We as parents never seem to give them enough. If they could have their inheritance now, many young hearts would take it without thought or question. The prodigal son was out of line to ask for his inheritance. Not only was he out of order, he was the youngest child. His father gave him his portion as he had asked him to do. The son went out, wasted his inheritance, and got down to nothing. He was at his lowest point. He was desperate, so he got a job feeding pigs. Jews weren't even allowed to touch pigs! He had fallen as low as he could go, even desiring food from the pig's slop. What a shame! This son came to his senses, went to his father, and asked for forgiveness.

    His father welcomed him home, gave him a robe, and had a feast for him. This is a beautiful example of God's love and grace for us, even when we do wrong. The first thing we must do as parents is train up our children the right way, so they will have a good foundation. Then, we can trust in God's Word and watch it come alive in them. The prodigal son's father was a God-fearing man who believed in God's Word. I can imagine that there were times that he may have wondered why his son was so selfish and disrespectful to him. He knew that he raised his son the best way he knew how. If we don't set the foundation by the Word of God, we have no room to complain to God when our children are taking over our homes. We must invite God into our lives as well as our homes. I don't know about you, but I need God in every aspect of my life. We have agreed, from the beginning of our marriage, to invite God into our home.

When things get out of order, we consult God for direction. We seek His direction through His Word and stand on His promise to us. I believe this is what the prodigal son's father did. He had given his son all he had to give him, material things and a spiritual upbringing. Life is not easy, and raising children is not easy. When we don't follow the standards that God has set for our homes, our homes can turn into a complete madhouse. Children disrespect and abuse their parents by cursing them out and fighting with them. That's not what God had in mind. I know that to be a fact.

He did say that we should not spare the rod. Why are we sparing the rod and expecting our children to fear us and to fear God? Some parents say, "I don't want my children to fear me". Let me tell you something. Fear brings respect. I respect God and fear His judgment. So, who sets the order in our homes, the government or God? I remember the saying, "It's better for parents to deal with their children at home than for them to go to jail". Now we have the law making it hard to discipline our children. It seems as if the law is on the youngster's side.

That same law has no problem shooting our children when they disobey the law and have or even appear to have a weapon. Don't get me wrong. I don't believe in abuse, but I believe in the Word of God. There's no way I would raise my children without the Word and the fear of God in me! Having raised them by the Word, my husband and I now stand on the Word of God. We all know that when our children are out of line; it disrupts our home.

Another disruption in our homes can come from our finances. It has been said that money is the root of all evil. What happens when we don't let God in on our finances?

CHAPTER 3

HANDLING OUR FINANCES

"I paid the cost to be the boss." Have you heard that before? I have many times. "No money, no honey!" Here's another one, "Don't play with my money". How about "Fifty, fifty?" The last is my favorite when it comes to marriage. My Uncle James used to say, "No fifty, fifty!!". In marriage, you must give all of yourself. The husband must be able to provide for his family. Now there's a song out called "All of Me" by John Legend. That song about sums up what my uncle has been saying for years. My uncle believed that the husband should be able to provide for his wife without depending on her half.

He would always ask me, my cousins, and other church members; "What's going to happen when you can't pay your half?". My cousin Tonya and I would just look at each other. Then my eyes would get big, and I'd look at her and say, "What?" Uncle James would say, "That's right. You may get sick and can't work." You might not be able to pay your half.

The Bible says that the wife is the helpmate. Uncle James made us understand that the husband depends on God to help him provide for his family, not his helpmate. If the husband can't work, sure, she will provide. Nowadays, many women must work to help provide for their family.

Times have changed, but the principles remain the same. There's a song that says, "There's No Half-Stepping!" God gave us His all. He paid the cost to be our boss with his life on the cross. We must give one-hundred percent to each other and to Christ. He is the head of our finances. I believe this was one of the reasons Abraham paid his tithes to Melchizedek, King of Salem. Abraham wanted to show that God was over his finances and worldly possessions. This should be true in our families. The Lord wants our first fruits. There are a lot of people who don't like to hear about paying tithes. I used to be one of those people. I grew up in a holy ghost filled, speaking in tongues, and sanctified church. My grandmother was on a fixed income, yet she paid her tithes before anything else. On the other hand, I felt like I didn't have much, so God would understand. I gave him what I wanted, when I wanted, and how I wanted. No set amount and no order. I believed that I needed all my money. "God will understand," I would always say. When I needed something, I always asked God for help. I have never been without. I've been down but not totally without.

Now I realize that we as Christians should take care of the house of God. The church has bills, just as we do in our homes. Some small churches don't have enough members or members paying their tithes to pay the bills of the church. The Lord has blessed me so much that I love to help others and support my church. I know that the more I give; the more He will give to me. Even when I was selfish, He kept on doing great things in my life.

This chapter is about finances, not tithes. In marriage, finances and tithes go hand in hand. The husband and wife must agree to pay tithes together

I've heard couples over the years saying, "My husband or my wife gives all our money to the church. That's why we don't have anything." When I got married I said, "Oh, we are going to pay our tithes?" We did too. We paid what we wanted to, when we wanted to, and how we wanted to. My husband had the same spirit that I had as a single parent. Robert and I are soul mates. Robert being the head of the household, would put our tithes in the envelope every Sunday. One day I asked him,

"How much did you put in the envelope?"

"I not telling you how much," he replied.

Can you believe it was less than a hundred dollars? We made more than a few thousand dollars a month, and there wasn't even a hundred dollars in the envelope. I began to watch and pray. Pray and watch. I did a lot of watching, and then I began to really pray. "Lord, please help my husband understand how important it is for us to pay our tithes. We need to pay our ten percent at least."

After prayer one day, God laid a question on my heart. Is it important for us to pay ten percent or to pay our tithes together, whatever the amount may be? I pondered on this question. I didn't know. I knew that was what I had been taught all my life. In fact, the Bible teaches us to pay ten percent.

Robert and I were driving home one Sunday afternoon after church. I had my head leaned back, listening to El Debarge's slow song called "A Second Chance". I heard Robert say, "Babe". I was lost in that song. I raised my head up, "Yes, Babe."

"What are the differences between tithes and offering?"

"An offering is what we give to the Lord just because, out of gratitude. Tithes are what we pay out of our income," I told him.

Then he said, "We talked about this in our newcomer's class today. We should give ten percent. For some people who haven't practiced the principle of giving ten percent, it might take some time."

I listened as he told me what he learned in newcomer's class. Then I replied, "What's important is that we pay our tithes together." There was the answer to the question that God laid on my heart. He nodded his head yes. I smiled and listened to the song that was on called "A Second Chance" by L. This was a secular song. Robert and I love to listen to nice, clean, slow music. I thank God for prayer and wisdom. I didn't fight with Robert about paying tithes. I just prayed about it.

Two people dealing with money together isn't always easy. It sure wasn't easy for us. We invited God into to our finances, and we were also accountable to each other. We focused on our house, not our friends. When it comes to finances, it can be hard to stay focused. Some women pay the bills in the home. In our home, Robert pays all our bills. I had the responsibility as a single mother. I was happy to let him deal with the bills. I do pay my credit card bills. When it comes to our finances, Robert and I just have to be honest with one another.

Sometimes, well, let me be honest, I swipe a lot! At the store, restaurants, and anywhere, that accepts debit or credit cards. Robert told me that I need to carry some money on me. It can be very painful when I see exactly how much money we both spend daily. It's more shocking knowing what we spent the money on. Swiping is great, easy, and convenient. The truth is, the more I swipe, the more unaccountable I am. Carrying money revealed some ugly truths that I didn't want to face. I was surely picking convenience over accountability by buying fast food and filling up my gas tank with the swipe of a card. I found out that I was unbalanced and so was my checking account. I found out that it cost too much to swipe and too much to do things my way, so I began to face the ugly truth head on. I started carrying some money and keeping track of my spending. I haven't packed my lunch yet to cut down on buying fast food, but I'm working on it. Swiping is just one area that affected our finances.

We still pray about it and ask God for wisdom on how we can cut back and not swipe so much. God did just that. Robert started packing and giving himself an allowance for the week. I'm still working on convenience and accountability. We have both made a lot of progress. Swiping will always be a part of our lives, but we are in control of our bank card. God is in control of us. We know that money can be the root to all evil.

When Robert and I got married, we made a mental list of the enemy's tactics on marriage, on the things he would use to come against us. Family, friends, children, in-laws, habits, and money all made the list. Our family was good. The children gave Robert respect. We had peace when it came to our in-laws, and we didn't have any outrageous habits. Money, that's where the enemy drew back his bow and arrow and took his best shot.

My husband and I had been friends ten years before we got married. When we started dating, we felt as if God had given us heaven on earth. We literally breathed each other's breath. When we slept at night, we slept face to face. While driving in the car, we would stop at every stop light just to kiss. We were caught up in each other. Nothing else mattered.

We had decided that we were going to include God in every aspect of our lives. We never intended on living together before we got married. I don't think any true Christian plans to live in sin. Robert and I found ourselves caught up in a situation. I was renting a house that went into foreclosure, so I had to move. It's a long story. However, we should have never moved in together before we got married, not even for a short while. We started putting our money together to pay bills. We were living as husband and wife, and we weren't even married yet. This caused us a lot of chaos. We tried putting our bank accounts together, as well as having our own accounts. We just couldn't seem to get it right. Not only were we dealing with managing money; my back had gone out, and I had to go on medical leave.

I trusted in God to provide for me. I still felt

like I had to work. I took any job I could to maintain my independence. I found out that the more I worked, the more my back stiffened up. I quit working and kept going to the doctors for treatment.

Meanwhile, Robert and I were still trying to figure out how we were going to handle our bank account. One of us wanted one account while the other wanted an account for the bills and separate accounts for each other. We weren't living the life that God had intended for us to live. We had done a good job of making a mess of things. We were indeed out of order. Our Father, Lord and Savior, came to our rescue.

First, we consulted Him through prayer. We asked for forgiveness for living in sin. We asked Him to help us with our finances and cleanse us of our wrong doings. Finally, yet importantly, we asked Him to forgive us for not including Him in our finances. After that prayer, God revealed to me why we should not have lived together, not even for a minute before marriage. My mind went back to how happy and carefree we were when we were dating. The only thing on our mind was how much we loved each other, not our bills or bank accounts. God wanted us to focus on the love part.

I understand now that God loves us so much that He wants us to enjoy whatever stage we are in our lives; single, engaged, or married. We were engaged trying to live as though we were already married. Later on in the family series, we will talk more about God's plan for us when we are single. I think it is amazing how God plans and puts thing together. He can't rule our lives unless we invite Him in. Thank God Robert and I invited Him in. We realized that we wanted to enjoy all that God has for us even in our engagement.

After we got married, we decided that we had become one, and our bank accounts would too. Nothing would come between us to divide us; not family, children, in-laws, habits, or money. The enemy has thrown us some tough blows and challenges in our finances. Some of the blows have knocked us down straight to our knees. When my mom passed away, I didn't know what to do. I thought my life was over, and that I would be living dead trying to pay for funeral debts, not knowing where the money was going to come from. Being the oldest child, I wasn't prepared for anything like that. I just had to lean on the Lord.

My mom took care of her affairs. She didn't leave my sister and I any debt. God worked things out. My mother used the wisdom of God and took care of her debts and the seeds that God gave her.

When it comes to money, my husband and I are learning to use the wisdom of God. We still have challenges today, but we love to see God meet our challenges and our needs. We have allowed Him into to our finances. Now we can proclaim the scripture that says I have never seen the righteous forsaking nor his seed begging bread (Psalm 37:25, KJV).

God honors His promises always. I mean always. On our six-year anniversary, we went to Deer Creek for two days. It was beautiful with nice scenery, hot tub, swimming pools, games, restaurants, gift shops, and a lounging area with a fireplace. We picked Deer Creek as one of our small anniversary trips. Every other anniversary we will take a big trip like a cruise or something.

When I booked our stay at Deer Creek, I booked the weather package, which included breakfast every day and twenty-five dollars towards dinner each day. Little did I know, we were going to need these meals. This was a getaway that I planned on not booking due to us buying a house, which was a short sale. Shorts sales can be long, so we had been saving up money for inspection closing cost and home insurance. Robert and I decided not to use credit cards until after we closed on the house. Talk about living on the bare minimum. We were, so we didn't have much money to spend at all. That first night at Deer Creek when we were at dinner, I had salmon, green beans, and a baked potato. All Robert wanted was chicken wings. Our bill came up to thirty dollars and some odd cents. We used our twenty-dollar coupon that came with the weather package with our bank card and also added a tip. The waitress came and collected our bill. "I'll be right back", she said. Robert and I smiled, shook our heads, and gave her a nod. "Okay," we both replied. In about five minutes, the waitress came back and told us that our card had been declined. "Do you have some other method of payment?"

"How could this happen?", I thought to myself. I remembered we had left our other cards at home, so we gave her our dinner coupon for the next day. This almost ruined our vacation. I asked Robert if he checked our account. He said no. "Did you buy something else?" I asked him. He was quiet. Then he replied, "I did pay on something". Right then, I knew it was something for me. "Let's enjoy our anniversary", he looked at me. "Please", he said.

"Okay, Okay!" I replied.

Later on that night, he got our box that we keep the cards in from our wedding, "Let's go by the fireplace, Babe." To the fireplace, we went. There were two chairs in front of the fireplace. Both of us sat in the chairs and rocked in front of it. While we were rocking, two couples came into the lounge to play cards. They pulled up two tables close to the fireplace and started playing cards.

"We can read these cards later", Robert said. Every anniversary we read each other the cards we received on our wedding day from family and friends. I sat in front of the fireplace, wondering why my husband would put money on an expensive gift for me knowing that we are buying a house. I told him that I wanted a tennis bracelet, but I changed my mind due to us buying a house. "Why would he still pay on it?" I thought to myself. Now we don't have any money to spend for two days until we get paid. There's no need to take money from elsewhere just to spend on a three day, two-night trip.

The longer I sat in front of the fireplace; I realized that God was already supplying all of our needs. My wants were just that, wants. Our meals were already paid for as long as we didn't go over twenty-five dollars. "Tomorrow I'll have chicken,

Lord willing," I thought to myself.

All things work together for the good of them that love the Lord. We are learning that the more we give, the more He gives to us. We have a heart for people; we love to give to others. As the Lord blesses us in our finances, we see that it is better to give than to receive. Dealing with finances can make a marriage strong or weaken a marriage. Robert and I had a great night. We took turns reading the cards, opened our sparkling cider, said we loved one another, and listened to our song "My Greatest Inspiration" by Teddy Pendergrass. Treating each other with respect in every area of our marriage is the only way to have a strong marriage. People say respect is something that we must earn. We must respect each other no matter what. This will bring us under subjection to the will of God to bring order to our home.

CHAPTER 4

HOW WE TREAT EACH OTHER

I thank God for my best friend Evelyn. We taught each other a lot about respect. In all the thirty years that we have been friends, we have never called each other out of our names. I'm not saying that we have always agreed, but we sure know how to agree to disagree. We have had some long deep discussions. Can you imagine two strong-willed women who believe that their point of view was right on any discussion? That was us, and neither one of us would waver. We could stay on the phone for hours going back and forth on whatever the subject was that we were discussing. Sometimes there would just be silence on the phone, I would say, "Are you there?" She would reply very sternly, "Yeah I'm here!"

Then everything would go completely silent. No words, not even the sound of the wind from our breath hitting the phone. We would hold the phone for a few short minutes, then one of us would say

"OK, I'll let you go." I believe we would hang up so fast that the click of the phone couldn't be heard. For us to achieve this, we had to hang up at the same time. Even when we were in each other's presence, we could agree to disagree and even get mad at each other.

I think she got mad at me more than I got mad at her. I can remember being about fourteen or fifteen years old spending the night over at each other's house and wearing each other's clothes. Wow! That was in the eighties when everyone just had to have a water bed and a Michael Jackson jacket. We would walk down the street with our boom box up against our ears just listening to the beat in the heat.

One day, Evelyn wanted me to see if I could stay the night. She called me and said, "Hey Fee, see if you can spend the night. My mom just bought me a new water bed."

My eyes popped out of my head! "What! Are you serious?" Meet me down the street in ten minutes. I got my clothes ready and down the street to Eve's I went. When the men came to deliver her water bed, I was right there. After they set up the bed, Evelyn's mom and dad told us to fill it up. I helped fill that water bed up as if it was my own. Evelyn and I put the sheets on the bed then we sat down on the bed and talked. As we talked I took out my pillow and sewing needle so I could finish sewing it for my homemaking class. With Michael Jackson's song "Lady of my Life" playing on the radio, we bobbed our heads to the music as I sewed. I thought we were in heaven when suddenly Evelyn's smile turned to a frown. I saw her taking her hands very slowly across the bed.

"Fee, Fee!"

I stopped sewing and put my sewing needle down and looked at her.

"THE BED IS GETTING WET" she shouted.

"OH NO!" I jumped up.

The next thing I know she grabbed my hand, then she slung it down towards the floor.

"LOOOK!"

I looked, and I couldn't believe my eyes! There sticking in the bed was a sewing needle. I had been sewing and using the bed as if it were a pincushion or something! I couldn't even see clearly; but before one tear could fall, Evelyn cautioned me not to worry. "I'll just tell my mom that it's a defect." She told me to put the sewing needle and pillow up. After I did what she told me to do, she began to scream. "Mom! Mom!"

Mom came running in, "What's wrong baby?"

"There's holes in this bed."

"WHAT! WHAT?"

Her mom screamed with some choice words to follow. Then her dad came running in.

"OH NO! OH NO!" he kept repeating himself.

"Calm down!" Mom told him. Then she grabbed Evelyn and told her not to worry as she reached for the phone to call the place where she bought the bed.

"You guys will have to sleep upstairs," she said. "They will bring you another mattress tomorrow."

I'm sure if her mom had of look at my face, she would have known that I put the holes in the water bed. I felt horrible, so I just kept quiet as if I was just as shocked as everyone else. Evelyn and I spent the rest of the night in silence. Our exciting day had turned into a nightmare. Yet silence was better than any words. I don't know if she called me any names in her head, but she held her composure enough not to let one-word slip out of her mouth.

That's just one example of how we've dealt with issues over the years. We can get mad at each other, then turn around help each other. What I've learned about respect through our friendship has helped me a lot in my marriage. I must say even though my husband is my best friend, I had to learn how to stay calm and fight fair.

I'm still learning his language. We have a different opinion when it comes to what name-calling is. I call my husband sweet and sour. When he's sweet, he's sweet. When he's sour, he's indeed sour. That's not name calling, is it? Or you must have a problem? What? These saying are all names as far as my husband is concerned. I must say my husband never passes judgment on me. He forgives me when I'm wrong, then he lets it go. When he's wrong, he'll apologize and then work on getting things right.

I on the other hand will sometimes say, "I'm sorry, but..."

There are no but's in sorry or if's in forgiveness. When I destroyed my best friend's water bed, she didn't speak to me for a couple of day's maybe, but she forgave me. She will always remember that day. The good thing about forgiveness is she never brought it back up.

Sometimes it's hard to forgive each other when we're hurting each other by our actions. Forgiveness is a choice not an emotion. Forgiveness is a gift from God. God's gifts are free whether we choose to live for Him or not, He still forgives us repeatedly. He's our prime example. In His Word, He calls us (mankind) his friend. The Bible teaches us that we should pattern our marriage after God's love for the church. We must show ourselves friendly first towards one another.

Remember the bracelets WWJD meaning "What Would Jesus Do"? When we're dealing with issues that affect our home, we should ask ourselves what Jesus would do? What is His plan for us? Are we treating each other like friends? Think friendship first. Loyal friends don't treat each other bad. Love and respect is a must in all relationships! In a marriage as well as single-parent household with one parent, God's way is always the best in everything. I don't understand why anyone would rather choose their way over God's.

My husband will get mad at me. When he's mad, he doesn't want to say I love you or for me to even touch him. He never stays mad long; he always forgives me right away. He never brings it back up again.

When I'm hurting because of something that I may have said to him, he lifts me up. He holds me in his arms and sees me as the wife he has valued to take care of even when I am not acting like his wife. This is what the Lord does for us also as His children. When we are wrong, He corrects us when we can't even admit that we are wrong, he chases after us, brings us to Him, and cleanses us through forgiveness love and kindness.

I know my way may seem right when it comes to dealing with our children. Robert and I both feel that we know how to handle children. Well, we have one child and three young adults. Let me tell you that statement couldn't be farther from the truth. I have run my mouth plenty of times, made wrong choices, thought wrong things, and been too hard when it comes to our children. Children must be treated with respect also. Sometimes we may even need to forgive them, or even ask for their forgiveness. They are a gift from God. Yes, they can push our buttons. However, when we nourish them with God's love, we help to mold and shape them into the will of God. We introduce them to the plan that He has for their lives. Justice isn't always the way when it comes to children, or young men and women. The Bible says that we should spare not the rod. Not kill them! What about meekness and love? How about patience? Raising children is by no means easy.

When our children grow up to be young men and women, they should be treated as such. We shouldn't go over to their house and dictate to them how they should live in their own home. Even though some of them are living in pure filth. Ask questions, offer advice, and try to help them. Do not invade their privacy. It can be painful watching our adult children make mistakes. God will see them through just as He did us. We must not threaten them if they don't do what we would like for them to do. We don't have to agree with them when they're wrong; if they're wrong, they are wrong. One day these same children will have children of their own. We want to be good examples to them, so they will be a good parent to our grandchildren.

Blessings have been passed down to the fifth generation. God honors His promises. Robert and I have two grandchildren, a granddaughter, and a grandson. Yes, we are young grandparents; they call us "Meme" and "Pa Pa". Now we love our children, but the Lord knows we love our grandchildren. We have stepped back and allowed our daughter to raise her children. We do give advice, directions, and encouragement. My granddaughter has to be redirected many times. She's very hyperactive. My daughter is hyperactive also. I'm used to dealing with hyperactive children. I have a lot of experience after raising my daughter. My daughter on the other hand doesn't have that much patience. My granddaughter is a bundle of joy; I don't like to see her get into trouble. I find myself telling her "Please listen to your mother, so you won't get into trouble".

When she does get in trouble and come to me, it hurts even more when I have to send her away and tell her again to listen to her mom. It's funny how she knows that I'm her mother's mom and looks to me to save her. She's learning quickly that what mom and dad says goes. Not even grandpa (The big dog) can save her. Now, she may obtain some mercy and grace by calling on Jesus. May is three-years-old, and she knows how to pray.

One day, she spent the night over at our house. The next day my niece came over. They were in the kitchen sitting at the table eating. May got up from the table and came into the front room tapped me on my leg, "Me-Me! You have to come here!" She grabbed my hand, and I followed her to the kitchen. There was salt all over the kitchen table from one end to the other. She looked up at me with a sincere look on her face. She walked down to the beginning of where the salt trail started on the table and said, "Me, Me", as she walked to the end of the trail she pointed, and said,

"LOOK I DID ALL OF THIS, all of it".

She pointed, and all I could do was look at her.

"I'M SO SORRY," she said as she just held my hand and looked at me. I couldn't believe it! I was so upset with her. When I looked at her pretty, little face, all I could say was, "OK, you have to clean all of it up!"

I told her to take her little hand and brush the salt into her hand little by little. Then, throw it in the trash.

"You can have your cousin help you; if you need me, come and get me. OK?"

I don't know if my little granddaughter

prayed that day or not. Grace, mercy, and the love of God is what saved her that day. Oh, yes, her pretty too! She was also honest. I could have very well punished her; she deserved it. She looked shocked herself. I believe she was exploring and didn't even know that the salt would pour out so fast all over the table. Just because she's my granddaughter that doesn't give me a right to treat her any way I want. I thank God for wisdom. I have done plenty of things in my life that didn't deserve the grace and mercy of God.

The Bible speaks of knowing to do right, but still doing wrong. When we know to do right, yet choose to do wrong, we're in the hands of God. He is a just God, yet He treats us with so much compassion and love. How we treat each other will determine how far we make it in life, in marriage, in family, and in business. People tend to think that we should treat people how they deserve to be treated. That's not what the Bible teaches us, we are to show love to each other in spite of their actions, which is not an easy task. We need instructions from the Word of God. Even with instructions, it's still hard.

We bought a house in a neighborhood where we became the minority. We live in a predominantly Caucasian neighborhood, with some Asian and people of Spanish descent. Our neighbor doesn't seem to like anyone who is different than her by race or disability. She will put people down and disrespect them. She talks about one neighbor's flaws to the other neighbor and shares another neighbor's issues with the whole neighborhood. I still respect her no matter how she acts and treat others.

Robert and I teach our children and grandchildren to love and respect one another, as well as others. No two households will raise their children the same exact way. That's OK! We all make mistakes the main thing is to have the same C.E.O. running our home. He is full of love and respect. We must treat our children and grandchildren with respect also. We need to do an assessment of our lives to see if there are any areas where we've fallen short in respecting others. In these areas where we find a lack of respect for someone, we need to find out why.

I used to find myself having a lack of respect for one of my colleagues. She was the kind of person who would say things and do the total opposite. Many times, I found her setting standards and going against them herself. I viewed her as unstable in all of her ways. I had very little words for her. I found it to be very hard to work with her. In fact, I was always uncomfortable working with her.

One day, she told me that whenever she spoke to me I never seemed to be happy. I told her that I used to love my job until we began working together. She looked at me and frowned. I realized that what I said had offended her. I really didn't care because it was the truth. Then I said to myself,

"Well, we do have to work together. How can we get along?"

I decided to discuss with her the things that had been bothering me that was affecting our work relationship. First, I apologized to her for not welcoming her pleasantly when she came to work. Then, I began the conversation by telling her what my issues were with her.

"Heidi, I don't like how you try to twist things around to work in your favor."

"What!" I don't know what you are talking about."

Heidi looked like she was choking on something.

"Heidi, I believe as a Christian you should be honest. When you say you're going to do something, do it. I don't like it when you turn things around, and then say, 'I thought you were going to do it', knowing very well that you said you were going to do it."

"Maybe I forgot! God forbid, I just wouldn't do that!"

"No Heidi, you have a habit of doing this all the time. I just want you to know that when you say you're going to do something and don't do it, I'm not going to do it for you! I want you to know I'm a great worker, anyone who has ever worked with me will tell you that I will go above and beyond my job requirements. I'm a leader, and a team player. I will not let you take advantage of me! When you need help, just ask. I would appreciate it if you asked me for help instead of twisting things around to make it look like I'm not doing my job in order for me to complete your job."

Even though Heidi was wrong, I was wrong for treating her unpleasantly. I don't like her character at all, but I will treat her with respect.

Even a murderer deserves respect. Wow, think about that! I believe murder is horrible, and a child molester is a disgrace. I wonder if the individual has committed a horrible crime, do I have a right to disrespect him or her? Can I spit on them because they are murderers and child molesters? In my opinion, a child molester deserves more than just to be spit on. He can be thrown under the jail, with the jail resting on his chest for the rest of his life. A child molester doesn't deserve to be treated good at all. That's my fleshly opinion, but that's not what the Bible says at all. Here's what the Bible says,

"And as ye would that men should do to you, do ye also to them likewise" (Luke 6:31, KJV PROSPECTIVE).

Today was a long day at work. I drove home from work, and my daughter was meeting me in the driveway. The first thing she said was "Mom?"

I said, "Yes, dear?"

She said, "You won't believe it!"

"What?"

"There's a ticket on your car!"

"What?!?"

"Yes, I saw the police in our driveway. I got scared because I didn't know what was going on. I called my cousin Malcolm; he told me to call the police. I did, and they said that one of the neighbors had called the police."

I got out of the car and grabbed the ticket. On the way to take my daughter to practice, I tried to drive and read the tickets. The more I drove, the angrier I became. I stopped at a red light; this gave me a chance to look at the tickets closely.

"Inoperable vehicle? What? What? What?!?" I just kept yelling. Then I screamed, "I can't believe it! We got a ticket on our car when it was parked in our driveway! Yeah right! I know who called the police; it was that Pat across the street. She is always doing something! Why doesn't she just leave us alone? We bought our house just like she bought hers, and we are not going anywhere."

I dropped my daughter off at her practice and turned around to drive back home. While driving, I called my sister Kate.

"Do you believe this neighbor, Pat, called the police about our car in the driveway."

"What? Are they crazy? What? Your car in

the driveway?"

"In our driveway, yes, that's right!" I told Kate with disgust.

It was true. My jeep liberty had been down for almost a month, but it hadn't even been a month yet. We were just about to get it fixed. I just couldn't believe the nerve of our neighbor. Pat just tries to find something to nitpick about all the time.

"Kate, you know what I'm going to do as soon as I get home? I'm going to park our expedition right in front of their house on their side, and I'm going to take our other car and park on the other side right in front of our house. You know they got mad when we parked in front of our own house, and she couldn't get out of her driveway. I can't believe people! I tell you I'm so mad! When Robert gets home, I'm going to tell let him know I'm not having this. This is not right!"

"OK," Kate said, "let me know if you need help. I will come over and park my big utility truck right in front of their house also."

I got off the phone with Kate and kept driving home. As I was driving, I began to think of what kind of example it would be if I parked my vehicle in front of the neighbor's house, if I made a big fuss outwardly about the neighbor calling the police. After all, it's just my assumption that Pat was the neighbor who called the police. I was just angry.

As a homeowner, I felt like I wasn't welcomed in the neighborhood, especially as an African American homeowner when the majority of the people on our street are Caucasian. I prayed. I drove home and begin to think how wrong it was for someone just to call the police on us about our car in the driveway when we don't bother anybody! We didn't do anything!

I began to think. Now, I know Pat doesn't like people with disabilities. She expressed that to me when we first moved into our house. So now, I'm really beginning to think that she just doesn't like anyone who is different than her. I started to get angrier and angrier! I thought Pat was just a racist, but it seemed to be much more!

I knew I wouldn't be an example if I did what my mind was telling me to do in anger, park my car in front of her house to try to affect her. After all, when we first bought our house, she told me she Googled me. She knew I was an author and a Christian. Now what kind of example would I be showing Pat if I did those things? Would my actions lead Pat to Christ? I thought to myself and answered my own question, "No".

If I parked my car in front of her house, she would get mad. This would not lead her to Christ. In fact, Pat would probably think that I am just like anyone else. That is not the image that I would want to portray, being a Christian woman, I didn't park our cars in front of Pat's house.

I thought long and hard that night and asked God to let me be an example to my neighbors. I asked Him to let my reaction in this incident be an example to my daughter who was watching my actions. I started looking at things differently. We stayed in a very nice neighborhood, and we got flyers on how to keep up your neighborhood. It always talks about reporting broken down cars, cars that are inoperable. Maybe this wasn't about race at all; it was just about Pat or whoever called the police wanting to keep up the property value on the houses in our neighborhood.

Whatever the case, their motive was not concerning to me anymore. I was just glad that I handled the situation in the right way, thanks to God. Dealing with this situation, I tried to look at the other person's point of view. It is not easy finding something positive in a very negative situation. I tried to teach my daughter (she's the last one in the home) to look at things at a different angle and not always try to think that someone is a gangster or trying to do something to her. I tried to teach her that there will be situations to where someone might just be plain wrong but that doesn't mean that we can make wrong choices too.

"But I say unto you, love your enemies, bless them that curse you, do good to them that hate you, and pray for them which despitefully use you, and persecute you" (Matthew 5:44, KJV).

Even though I don't agree with the actions of my neighbor, co-worker, or even a murderer and child molester; I still should treat them right like the Bible teaches me to. Only a Christian can live by these principles, someone trying to live Christ-like by following God's Word, the Bible. The Bible doesn't condone people living or doing unjust things, but it teaches us love no matter what and that it's not easy to treat those who have offended us with love.

"If you love those who love you, what credit is that to you? Even sinners love those who love them" (Luke 6:22, NIV).

I know it's far-fetched to compare how I treat my co-worker, neighbor, or boss at work to how I would treat a murderer or a child molester. I am always searching my heart and trying to paint a picture for myself of how Christ would want me to treat others. I know no matter how I feel about others, I must treat them right. When I have encounters with others who are not displaying the characteristics of Christ, I challenge them. I challenge myself daily to live by the principles of Christ. I know I can't change others, but I do believe that I can set an example for others.

We have a no excuse rule in our family. That rule has carried us a long way. By holding each other to our no excuse rule, we help one another by being accountable for our own actions. Knowing that we are responsible for our own actions, we can't blame anyone else for the choices that we make. We choose to treat people right no matter what. We are accountable for our own actions. When a person is not accountable for their actions, that means they will treat people anyway they want to. People seem to do this when they have no one in their lives to hold them accountable for their own actions. These people seem to care a lot about how others treat them with no regard to how they treat others.

My cousin Lisa made me aware that her husband never had any good role models when he was growing up. She said he may have had people who he looked up to, or had seen good men on TV; but looked at them as fiction. After all, to him, no one has a family like The Cosby Show. The family that he lived in was more like Good Times, without a good male role model. "DJ" is what everyone calls her husband. DJ has been in and out of trouble since he was young. He came from a single-parent home with a mom who loves him dearly. His mom was always trying to guide him in the right direction. She gave him words to live by, but no accountability. I'm sure, as with many young men in his neighborhood, DJ was angry. Angry that he had to live in a household without a father. Being the oldest boy in the home, I'm sure he felt a sense of control. He was a leader already, the man in the home. How could he be the man in the home when he was just a boy? Yet, he had so much responsibility and no male influence or guidance.

I've known Jack for over seventeen years, and he has never shown respect for women, or his wife. He treats her like crap. He has more excuses than the law will allow as to why he can't provide for his family. He's a felon, so he can't get a job. He sits at home being a "daddy mom" while his wife works and takes care of the family.

A few years ago, he had surgery on his hand which left him considered as disabled and not able to work. Although he has never greeted me in a disrespectful way, he is a bad example for his family. He doesn't seem to feel like he has any responsibility to his wife or his children. Lisa believes it's because he doesn't have anyone to hold him accountable for his actions. Now, his brother tries, but he's younger than him. I think Jack may feel like he has been dealt a bad hand, and he just playing it out the best way he knows how. There's no excuse for how he treats his family.

Unfortunately, in this life we only get one deck of cards. God is our dealer, and there are no do-overs. We can't play our hand out and wait for the dealer to deal us another hand. In a card game, we can't ask the dealer how to play our hand, because he is in the game just like we are. He or she just dealt the cards. In life, we can ask our dealer for help. God is the one who gave us life, and He has the instruction on how to live this life. There is no do-overs, but the way we live this life will determine where we spend our eternity. Hell, or heaven, one way in and no way out. Heaven is one way in through Christ. The good thing is that once we make it in, we are there for eternity. Hell has many ways to get there, but no way out!

Jack didn't have anyone to hold him accountable when he was growing up. He has a lot of excuses as to why he is not a good leader for his family. No matter what his life has been like in the past, he must read God's Word and learn how to treat his family and others.

CHAPTER 5

WHEN DO WE SAY WE'RE SORRY

I find myself asking the question, "Is it okay not to say, 'I'm sorry', when getting into disagreements with family members?" For me, a disagreement is a disagreement, and there is no need for an apology. On the other hand, sometimes we may have disagreements with family members and they may be offended without anyone knowing it. Communication is the key. It is never my intent to offend anyone in my family through a disagreement, but I will never know if that person is offended unless they tell me. Many times, we take for granted that they know when we are offended, but that's not always the case. Most of the time when I get into it with my relatives, I just brush it off, especially when there is a disagreement. Now if I feel like I have been offended by one of my family members personally, then I will let them know.

I'm learning to try to look at the intent of the person's heart who may have offended me. If I know that person wants the best for me, then I will try to look past hurtful words that they may have spoken to me. If I feel like every time I have a conversation with that person it is always negative without any positive words of encouragement, then I will limit my conversations with them. I feel like as an adult it is my responsibility to guard my heart and keep positive people in my life. We may not always agree; but if their goal is to help me grow, then it's a relationship worth keeping. I can be very opinionated. When I have an opinion that I feel strongly about, I will stick to it. When it comes to my children, I realize that they are adults now. Although I may not agree with their opinions, I understand they have a right to their own opinions. I have taught my children to be respectful and mindful of me as a parent when it comes to their opinions. Now, my son on the other hand is teaching me that not everyone likes constructive criticism. Out of love, we should be mindful of people's feelings. I believe that the intent of my heart has always been to be mindful of other's feelings. I don't believe that in my conversation it comes across that way. I have been working on this; sometimes it may take me letting the other person repeat to me what it is that they hear me saying. Sometimes the message that I am trying to relay to them is not the same message they hear. When I realize that they are getting the wrong message, then I will apologize.

I have different relationships with different people in my family. Now my sister, we have been having disagreements since we were younger. We will argue and disagree until the sun goes down. Most of the time, I must admit there are no apologies. Sometimes, I will even hang up the phone if we're on the phone. I will say, "Okay, you're yelling" or "We're not getting anywhere, so I'm going to hang up". When the conversation continues, then I'll hang up. I feel like it's my responsibility not to sit on the phone and have a dispute with someone that's not going to be resolved. If we talk later on and she makes me aware that I offended her, I usually apologize by saying, "I'm sorry if I hurt your feelings". I know that my sister feels like I shouldn't hang up on her because I'm her sister. We share different opinions, so I will apologize. I think it is rude for someone to hang up on someone just because they disagree. For me, if I'm on the phone and someone is yelling, my solution is to hang up or leave; and it doesn't matter if they are a family member or not. I just think that's the mature thing to do. Now if it wasn't a family member and I felt like the person was being rude by yelling and disrespecting me, most likely I wouldn't even continue a relationship with them. There is a difference between yelling and talking very loudly to get one's point across. I, for one, can stand firm talk without yelling and get my point across. I believe that yelling will get you nowhere; so, when a person is yelling or screaming, they will get nowhere with me.

I have learned a lot from my family, and I am still learning things. I do know that I place my husband under higher standards than other family members. When my husband and I have a disagreement, I always expect him to apologize. When it comes to my husband, my feelings are always hurt in a disagreement. Now when we were friends, we could just disagree all day long just like my sister and me. That wouldn't bother me and didn't bother me until we got married. Even though we're still friends, I don't know what it is, but being in love has made me sensitive. No one can hurt my feelings like my husband. All he has to do is disagree with me. There's a saying that says you "Never have to say you're sorry" or "Don't say you're sorry because you're not a sorry person". There is scripture on being sorry found in Psalms 38:18 or 2 Corinthians 7:9-10. We were taught through the Bible to be sorry for our sins. Sins are wrong doings and offenses to others. Being sorrowful will let us know the difference between right and wrong.

CHAPTER 6

RESTORING OUR BROKEN FAMILIES

What if we didn't start our family on the foundation of God? Maybe we did base our home by the foundation of the Word of God; but somewhere down the line, we decided to go by our own guidelines or the world's guidelines. Fixing our broken families is not our jobs. This job belongs to God. All we have to do is give Him permission to fix our family. Once we do that, we must begin to seek after His will for our family, admit that we believe God's way is the best, and trust Him to do the rest. Then, get ready for the journey. God will cleanse us from all of our past mistakes. We must do this through prayer, by acknowledging that we can't run our homes on our own.

The Bible teaches us that we can do all things through Christ Jesus that strengthens us. Through Christ, He is the key to fixing our broken families. God doesn't operate on dictatorship, so we have to acknowledge that we are indeed His children by accepting His will for our lives. We find His will for our lives through His Word, the Bible. We agree in prayer that we can do nothing without Him. Then, we search our hearts to find out what areas we have left Him out. If it's with our children, we invite Him in by asking for His help. This may not be an easy process, but it's necessary. Remember, He needs our permission to be the C.E.O. of our lives.

Some of us haven't taught our children respect, love, or honor. I would like to believe that we all as parents have; but without God, we aren't successful. I know I'm not, that's why He's my guide. My husband and I both seek God when it comes to raising our children. I must say we have had to go back to the beginning from time to time ourselves. My youngest daughter is cute as a button they say. No, she's really a great kid. She's almost fourteen, and we have had some days where she seems to forget what respect is. So, believe it or not, we must go back to the basics. I remind her that the Bible said to obey them that has rule over her, and to honor your father and mother that your days may be long. I ask the question; how can you honor us if you don't respect us? It's up to my husband and I to make sure she has a clear understanding of respect.

One of My favorite lines my husband loves to use is, "No two for one". She's good for that. When I tell her to do something, she always has something to say. Then I reply to her, "Did I ask you a question?" Of course, she gets mad. I don't care. I am determined to teach her to obey us without questioning us. It's work being a parent. Sometimes it may seem easy to just ignore what our children do and say. That's not what the Bible teaches us.

The Bible says to train up our children the way that they should go and when they're old they will not depart. This means we can't let up on our children. We must reinforce what we have taught them. I had to apologize to my daughter for not enforcing the same guidelines on her that I did with my older three children. They have grown up with a chore list posted on the refrigerator. I noticed that she was getting by with a lot of things that the older children didn't. They never ate a lot of fast food either. This one will call me on my way home from work and ask me to pick her up some Chipotle or McDonald's. I will just say "OK"; and before I realize it, she's getting what she wants. My older children only ate out on special occasions.

My daughter also tries to keep up with the latest technology, from laptops to tablets. Whatever she can get from my husband, she tries to get. I was a single parent a while before I got married. When I got married, she was six years old. She's the youngest. I realize that we have been doing her a disservice by not giving her a chore list and buying her too much fast food. I admit that it's my fault about the fast food. I'm a working mom, so sometimes I'm just tired when I get off of work. I have asked God to forgive me for not enforcing the guidelines that we have set in place in our home through His Word.

Now, I don't just tell our daughter to clean her room; I make sure that she knows what her responsibilities are. My husband and I will make sure she is doing her chores. I realize that she is a teenager, yet still a child. Left to herself, she will indeed self-destruct. She will come home from school, do her homework, watch TV, and get on the computer or her tablet. That's all she'll do without me or Robert following up. We show her that we love her by not leaving her to do her own will. Much like God does with us. What an example He is! I don't know what type of mom I would be without Him. I've learned a lot about children through reading His Word. When we teach them how to obey us, they will love and respect us. When they respect us, they will in turn honor us. What a blessing to have our children respect, love, and honor us! I love the honoring part.

It's a blessing being able to watch our girls grow up to be young women and seeing our son as a young man. It makes us both proud parents. Hearing them minister to other young people, passing down what they have learned from our household, is an honor to us and to God. I thank God for His grace and love. When a home is in disarray, it can be because of many things, not just our children. How about ourselves? Leadership in the home, finances, or outside invaders can all cause a home to be out of order. These are just a few things.

Order in the House is only one in part of a series. Sometimes we are our worst enemy. How do we fix ourselves if we are out of line in our home? Husband, wife, single man, or woman? I always say we must go back to the beginning. The Bible says that in the beginning was the Word and the Word was God and the Word was with God. We need God. I can remember a song that the older people used to sing in church when I was younger.

"I need thee every hour. I need thee Lord. Bless me now my Savior. I come to Thee."

They would just keep repeating those words over and over. I would feel the Holy Spirit stirring up inside of me. There's nothing good in us; we will make mistakes, all of us. If we ourselves fall short of the glory of God, we have to repent then change our ways. Some of us can be so stubborn at times. Why prolong the process when Christ is waiting to direct us? We commit ourselves to Him in prayer by taking full responsibility for whatever position we have taken in our homes. That means we should not be slacking as mothers and wives by doing what we want. The Bible also says there's a way that seems right to a man but such is destruction. Give it to God, whatever it may be. Some feel as if we are grown, and we can do what we want. How can that be if we are children of God?

We should choose to live by the example set by the Word of God. Mothers should be mothers. Our daughters are not our friends or sisters, so this means we won't approve of everything they do. We need to marry God-fearing men and don't accept anything less. Women who are single should be women their children can mirror after. I know it's not easy being single. Remember, I was a single parent at one time. If you are a single woman, you need to date honorable men. Don't let your daughters see you with men who don't respect, love, and honor you. I remember before I got married, I wouldn't let any guy that I was dating meet my children, even in my hay days when I used to go out. Yes, I was in between churches; so even though I grew up in church, I had my hay days. I had a couple of boyfriends other than my children's fathers. My children have never seen men in my bed except for their fathers and my husband. I knew, even when I was out of the will of God, that I had to lead by example. I was particular about who I let around my children. Thank God I never had a man beating me or disrespecting me. I, on the other hand, have thrown beer out of my refrigerator and smashed it on the concrete. I was serious about not having drinking around my children. I didn't drink in front of them; no one else did either! I told God a long time ago; I said, "God I may not be perfect, yes, I had kids before getting married. Please God, whatever you do, don't let me marry no fool". He answered my prayer. He will answer yours too.

Only you know what area you're out of line in. I urge you to give it to God so your home can be blessed by God. Women aren't the only ones that need order. There are many homes without a leader, even in marriages. A wife can't make a husband lead. Stop trying to make your husband lead the home. Pray that he will let God direct him. Men must be the leader in the home. Men, God has placed you as the head of the house. You should not be placing that burden on your wife. It is a burden to your wife if you're not leading your household, unless she wants to be the head of the household. Then, you really have some problems, but there's still no problem that God can't handle. Always go back to the beginning and start with God.

If you don't know how to lead, ask for His help. The Bible teaches husbands to love their wives as Christ loved the church and gave His life for her. Follow Him and the leader He is. He bears our burdens, corrects us with love by cleansing us through his Holy Spirit, and He draws us to Him to offer us grace and mercy. What a gift, husbands must draw the family through love, bear the burdens of the wife, and cleanse her.

Don't be afraid to lead your home by the Word of God. Your sons will grow up to be good men who love and respect their wives and children. Your daughters will grow to have good judgment and marry good men. They will be blessed wherever they go. This is a step in the right direction by leading your home by the will of God. Not only will your children have good judgment, but they will also learn respect. Men can be leaders in the home by leading their children and wives. People are taught to depend on leaders. Your wife and children need to know that they can depend on you. You depend on God, as they depend on you and God to get them through life. Men, if you are not being the leader in your home ask God for forgiveness, then your wife. Seek God on how you should lead your family. You must lead by His direction to receive His blessings for your family. Let your wife know that from this day forth, you have made a vow to God to take full responsibility for the family that He has given to you. You must understand that if you haven't been leading your home, you have caused your whole family to be out of order. Your wife may have taken control of things and have counted you out on making decisions. Have you noticed your children not coming to you for direction or advice, or your wife not directing them to you? If so, God can fix your situation. He will honor your prayer and vow to Him to be responsible for your family. You must have patience with your wife and children as they go through the process of learning that they can trust and depend on you as you seek God's will for your family.

During this process, you will need to share with your wife your fears and weaknesses. She is your helpmate. She can go before the Lord in prayer concerning those areas. You also need to pray for your wife and children. I can tell you, it's not always easy for women to trust their husbands to lead. Think about it this way, the Bible tells us to trust in the Lord with all our hearts and lean not to our own understanding. Do we always trust in Him?

I know there have been many times that I have lacked in this area. Instead of waiting on the Lord, I have tried to fix things. Understand that waiting is trusting in God. I believe if it's hard for some of us to trust God, it's safe to say that it's also hard for some of us to trust our husbands when they make decisions concerning the family. They will make mistakes. I know there's been times when my husband has made a decision that I didn't agree with. I have gotten mad, but God has also shown me through pray that I haven't always agreed with Him either.

I found out through my Christian walk that God knows what's best for me. As my husband trusts God, he must learn from God how to lead us as a family, not from me. I know that he values my opinion and has our family's best interest in mind when making a decision in our home. Knowing he loves God and us makes it easier to trust the decisions he makes. Getting the order together helps him be able to lead our home. Having God as our C.E.O. is number one. Believe me, if my husband ever gets out of line in his authority, I know who to go to. Women, if your husband has not been leading your home and is now trying to be the leader, stand with him in prayer. Be his helpmate, forgive him, and allow him to lead. God will be pleased with you. He will allow you to be a tool in others' lives, and He will show His word is real by showing His power in your lives. Others will want to know what caused the change in your marriage.

We can live a victorious life right here on earth by obeying God and letting Him lead our lives! If you are a single man or woman, remember the Lord Jesus Christ is your head. Follow the same steps above, and God will indeed restore your family back to the original design and plan for your family.

CHAPTER 7

A FAMILY DESIGNED BY GOD

What does a family designed by God look like? I know that it doesn't look perfect. Our family certainly isn't perfect.

God knows that there's nothing perfect or good in man naturally except by His Holy Spirit. He has given us tools in His Word on how we should build our families. The Bible says that on this rock I will build my church and the gates of hell will not prevail. He tells husbands to love their wives even as He has loved the church. What a comparison the wife to the church! If we build our house by the foundation of God, then we have the same promise. That's the beginning of designing a family by God's standards. The Word of God is the rock for our family. When we follow the Word of God for our families, we shield our household from destruction.

"Unless the LORD builds the house, its builders labor in vain. Unless the LORD watches over the city, the watchmen stand guard in vain, and take responsibility for our own sin" (Psalms 127:1).

The enemy will try everything in his power to come up against us. Marriage is one of the first covenants with God. We talked about going back to the beginning in previous chapters; well, here we go again. Adam and Eve were our example of a family design by God. Guess what, they messed up! They disobeyed God.

We can still have a family designed by God today. No, we are not going to go back to the Garden of Eden to start over! We must obey God; that's number one in designing our family by God. It's not easy, not at all. We must sacrifice some things to stand on the principles of the Lord. You may be standing alone at times. It may mean going against what others are doing in the world.

My oldest daughter used to get mad at me when I would always ask to see the books she had to read for school. While looking through some of her books in middle school, I discovered that there were curse words in some of them. I was surprised and demanded that she didn't read those books. She replied,

"Mom, they feel like we are in middle

school now, and we can take a few curse words."

Yes, standards are changing in our world. Do God's standards change? No, we must not waiver either.

What else happened in the Garden of Eden? Let's see, after Adam and Eve disobeyed God, they tried to cover themselves. They were naked, oh my! We should confess our sins and deal with them quick, so we can remain in good standings with Christ. We can't let the enemy fool us and shame us into believing that all is lost due to sin. Christ died on the cross for our sins He redeemed us with His blood. He never changed the order for our lives; He just took us in a different direction. We were created to live forever in one body in the garden.

In the beginning, He created man, then woman, from the rib of man. He created them to live free of pain and suffering and to live in the garden forever. I imagine that garden was like paradise with no evil; but only peace, happiness, and free will. He gave Adam and Eve the choice not to eat of the tree of knowledge. He knew if they ate of the tree, they would die for eternity. He chose to die on the cross, so we may live for Him forever not in this body but our heavenly body. The Bible says neither death nor the grave can hold us. We need to obey Him and confess our sins.

Now, Adam didn't even take responsibility for his own sin. Some of us may feel like it's impossible to do so if Adam failed. He did fail, but because of the grace of our Savior, we have the power of the Holy Spirit. We can choose to take responsibility for our own sin. No more "I'm like this because my mom or dad made me like this". We all will experience some unpleasant things in this life. We must choose not to be a victim or a repeat offender. When we do this, we start to live the way God intended for us to live. In order to live this way, we need a lot of prayer. Most Christians know that. Are they doing it?

We were not praying together as often as we should have been. We prayed when we went to church, but I can't give you a number on how many times we prayed at home. Praying together brings couples and families closer to God. When we pray together, we open ourselves up to God and each other. We speak about what's on our hearts and minds.

It's not easy for a lot of men to pray out loud. Some men may feel like they have to say some long, earth-shattering prayer. When my husband and I got married, he had a tough time praying aloud. In the beginning of our marriage, I always started the prayer by focusing on thanking God first, and then I would ask for forgiveness for my shortcomings. I would pray for protection for our children. It's not easy for a lot of men to pray out loud. I believe they think it shows that they are weak and need God's help.

I like being a woman and that women are called the weaker vessel in the Bible. I said before that men have to be weak also if we women are the weaker vessel. When I pray, I try to follow the order of prayer demonstrated in "The Lord's Prayer". First, I acknowledge God as my Father and Lord now and forever. I then pray to be a part of His kingdom to come. I ask for provision for our family and thank Him for all that He has done for us already. I pray to avoid temptation, and to be delivered from all evil, knowing that the Lord has all power and His kingdom will last forever. I pray for my husband to receive direction for our family and for God to reveal His plan to him. I pray for his strength and health. I pray that God protects him and that whomever he meets will be changed because of the glory of God seen through him. I pray that he changes the atmosphere everywhere he goes, and that he will have favor with God and man. I ask God to keep his heart strong and pure, and that he may continue to stand boldly for what is right. I want the power of the Holy Ghost to overtake him. Let the words of his mouth be acceptable in the eyes of the Lord. I pray that he will always acknowledge the Lord Jesus Christ as his Savior and Redeemer.

We can't have the family that God intended us to have without prayer. Through prayer, we embrace God and usher in His presence into our home and into our lives. The Bible tells us we have not because we ask not. The Word of God also said that He will give us the desires of our hearts. I know you may be thinking God knows and sees everything. Yes, He indeed does, but He is waiting for us to come to Him with all our needs and desires. His Word said that He will not withhold any good thing from us. The good thing is, if our desires are not pure or may lead us into sin, He will change our desires by the renewing of our minds and hearts.

"Do not be conformed to this world, but be transformed by the renewal of your mind, that by testing you may discern what is the will of God, what is good and acceptable and perfect" (Romans 12:2).

I wanted my husband to lead the prayer because he is the head of our household. My husband shared with me that he had never prayed with someone other than church, or on occasion when his family had prayer in the home growing up.

I guess on holidays and at dinner time. Praying with his family was very new to him. Realizing that I am his helpmate, I kept praying until he felt comfortable. I encouraged him to share with God the desires of his heart for our family. Praying together brings us closer together. Prayer means being intimate with God, and each other. It's a give and take thing, we open our hearts to Him and each other sharing intimacy with God through prayer will bind us together. The Bible tells us that,

"What God has joined together, let no man put asunder" (Mark 10:9).

This is so huge to me. This scripture leads me to believe that through prayer believing that God has joined us together, nothing shall separate us from God or each other. We choose to pray and allow God to direct our lives. When the Bibles says that which God has joined together, let no man put asunder. I believe that means me. I must continue to stand on the promises of God no matter what things look like.

Robert and I have decided that we are indeed

stuck with each other. This doesn't mean the we won't have storms, test, trails, and sometimes tribulations. We continue to give these things to God in prayer. We take the things that we have learned and are learning to God in prayer. God will help us apply these principles to our life. Don't believe the lie that God doesn't have a design for the family in this day and time. His design for our family started with the Word and will end with the Word.

After reading previous chapters if you're still having a hard time following the design or figuring out what the design is, start with the following Ten Commandments:

1. You shall have no other Gods before me.

2. You shall not make graven images or idols.

3. You shall not take the LORD'S name in vain.

4. Remember the Sabbath day.

5. Honor thy father and thy mother.

6. You shall not kill.

7. You shall not commit adultery.

8. You shall not steal.

9. You shall not bear false witness against your neighbor.

10. You shall not covet.

Read and memorize these commandments. Study them with your family. Hide them in your heart to help keep you from sin. We use His Word as our guide. In prayer, God will reveal His love for us; *In His Word, we learn how to love each other.*

CHAPTER 8

LOVE IS A CHOICE

The world says that love means never having to say you're sorry. What does the Bible say?

"If I speak in the tongues of men or of angels, but do not have love, I am only a resounding gong or a clanging cymbal. If I have the gift of prophecy and can fathom all mysteries and all knowledge, and if I have a faith that can move mountains, but do not have love, I am nothing. If I give all I possess to the poor and give over my body to hardship that I may boast, but do not have love, I gain nothing" (Corinthians 13, NIV).

"Be devoted to one another in love. Honor one another above yourselves" (Romans 12:10, NIV).

In these two scriptures, you can see there is a great need for love. It's impossible to love each other without forgiveness. In order to remain in peace and in love, sometimes we may have to say that we're sorry. I myself can be stubborn at times, but because of the love that I have for my husband, I will apologize. In spite of what you may think, love is more than just some emotion that we can't control. The Bible commands us to love one another.

"A new commandment I give unto you, that ye love one another; as I have loved you, that ye also love one another" (John 13:34, NIV).

We must decide to follow God's Word. I guess that's why people in the world will say that it's a thin line between love and hate. Maybe some people have realized that without love, hate is forever present. Love and hate don't coincide together. You can't love and hate someone. You either love them or hate them.

Christ loved us so much that He gave Himself for us. He suffered, bled, and died. He put us first above His own fleshly needs when He suffered physical pain in a body of flesh. Think about it! He knew that He would endure pain, yet He remained on the cross for our sins.

In marriage, we will go through a lot of trials and tribulation. It's not always easy to love each other. The enemy wants us to believe that love is painful, and it costs too much. Love is not painful at all. When we love each other on earth, we will experience pain together. But love will never cause pain. In fact, love is what frees us from hurt and all harm.

When Christ died for our sins, He did it out of love. Love didn't hurt Him at all. The pain He endured on the cross came from the hate of carnal men's hearts, who wanted to destroy him. There's a song that people in the world used to sing, the words to the song are, "If only you knew how much I do love you. If only you knew how much I do need you."

If only they knew how much Christ loved them and how much they needed Him, would they have crucified Him? He went through pain because of hate. He chose to lay down His life for our sins because of His love for us. He was God in the flesh. He could have chosen to come down from that old rugged cross; but instead, He prayed for them saying, "Father, forgive them for they know not what they do."

Love does cost us something, putting others needs before our own. Marry someone who follows Godly principles, so you won't get cheated. If each of you is trying to fulfill each other's needs, then you're equally being in love. Robert is good at putting me first. He had to learn to do this, which was difficult being that he has always been a loner. I'm sure our Father in Heaven is proud of him. He has managed to put me first, even with the smallest thing.

We have a restaurant here in Ohio called Rooster's Chicken. Rooster's has chicken wings cooked in special Rooster's sauce. Man, you talk about a struggle putting each other first! I don't know. Is chicken a need or a want? I seem to always want the last piece of chicken. We will look at each other; it will be so quiet that you can hear a pen drop. My mouth will be watering, and you can probably see my heart pounding across the room. "Please Lord, I need that piece of chicken," I will say to myself.

Then my husband will say, "Babe, do you want this piece?"

As I reach to grab the chicken, I will say, "Are you sure you don't want it?"

"Go ahead!"

"Thank you, babe."

Giving up the last piece of chicken may be small, but it still shows a lot of love.

My husband continues to love me as Christ loves the church. We share everything; sharing cars is a task though. We do believe what is his is mine, and what's mine is his. Now, I have a jeep, and he has an expedition. Both cars belong to us. Every winter for the last two years, I have been stuck driving the expedition, because the heat is not flowing right in the jeep. Sometimes I just don't like to share. My jeep has heated seats and memory program positioning. It was designed just for me. Robert tried several times to get the heat in the jeep fixed to no prevail. It still doesn't have enough heat for me, so we have switched cars. He must love me to be driving in a cold car in the winter. Robert made the decision to let me drive the expedition. I'm sure he would rather be driving the expedition instead of the Jeep.

The Bible teaches us to love one another. It doesn't say love each other when we feel like it or when things are going our way. We decide to love each other not based on feelings or situations. We love each other no matter what the day may bring. We will get angry with one another from time to time. The Bible tells us in Ephesians 4:26 to "be angry, but sin not".

It is a sin not to love each other. This is a commandment from God. I love to pick with Robert when he's mad at me. I'll say, "Sweet, are you mad at me?"

"I am," he'll sternly say.

"Well, can I have a kiss?"

"No!" he'll say as he walks away.

I'll follow him, "Why not, don't you love me?"

"Yes, but I don't want to kiss you!"

"Why not?"

"Because! I'm maaaad!"

Is that taking love for granted or what? Oh well, he doesn't stay mad long. I can't stand it when he's mad at me. Chances are, I will apologize, and he will accept my apology quickly. Love is powerful. If we are followers of Christ, His love for us is even more powerful. The Bible tells us we should let nothing and no one separate us from the love of

Christ.

"Who shall separate us from the love of Christ? shall tribulation, or distress, or persecution, or famine, or nakedness, or peril, or sword? As it is written, For thy sake we are killed all the day long; we are accounted as sheep for the slaughter. Nay, in all these things we are more than conquerors through him that loved us. For I am persuaded, that neither death, nor life, nor angels, nor principalities, nor powers, nor things present, nor things to come. Nor height, nor depth, nor any other creature, shall be able to separate us from the love of God, which is in Christ Jesus our Lord" (ROMANS 8:35-39).KJV

We must love God, each other, and our children. Yes, in that order! God should be first, then our mate, and followed by our children who are God's gift to us. Prayer, love, and forgiveness go hand in hand. We need them all.

CHAPTER 9

FORGIVENESS

Forgiveness frees us from the hate that has been imposed on us by our offenders. It gives us control in situations where we feel hopeless. When someone has caused us pain and we hurt them in return, we feed into negative energy. We can't change the family that God has allowed us to be in. We are to love each other in spite of how we feel. In our marriage, we need to forgive each other quickly, so the pain won't resonate and cause a scare hard to heal, which is the long-term effect of unforgiving. I'm not saying whenever someone does us wrong, they hate us. Unforgiveness can cause us to hate and live an unfulfilled life. That's why it's very important to choose to follow God's plan for our lives. By choosing the right mate, our family will be prosperous.

When we do things to offend each other, we have a choice to let it fester or resolve things quickly. When we don't deal with uncomfortable situations in our home right away, we allow the enemy to move into our house and become a resident. I don't know about you, but we are not having any free loaders in our home. We will not invite the enemy into our home.

I spoke a little about forgiveness in previous chapters, but we need to explore forgiveness more when it comes to our families as a whole. In the fleshly bodies that we're living in, we will be tried and tested. It is so easy to get even when we have been offended by someone including our mate. Forgiving is a process. The process can be painful when your mate of however many days, months, or years does something to offend you. Some things do take time; through the love of Christ, we learn how to forgive each other.

"If you forgive anyone his sins, they are forgiven; if you do not forgive them, they are not forgiven" (John 20:23, NIV).

"And whenever you stand praying, forgive, if you have anything against anyone, so that your

Father also who is in heaven may forgive you your trespasses" (Mark 11:25, ESV).

Some may deal with big issues that may require help from a pastor or a counselor. Remember, marriage is a covenant. Whoever married you, pastor or judge, has agreed the two of you should be together. It is so important to have good people in your corner to help you deal with difficult issues that affect the family. People in the ministry should be able to guide you by the Word of God.

As you go through the process of forgiveness, you may feel overwhelmed. Forgiving your mate when they've hurt you is hard. God knew that it wouldn't be a simple task. Remember the story of a man in the Bible who had a wife who kept leaving the home and sleeping with other men. The Bible tells us God doesn't want us to divorce; but if one commits adultery, we are free to divorce. This is about forgiveness. This man could have very well put his wife away by divorce. He decided to go after her and bring her home. The Bible doesn't tell us this, but I'm sure he experienced a lot of ridicule for this. People probably thought that he was crazy. I'm sure his family could care less if he brought his wife home. This woman didn't bring honor to his name at all. Why did he stay with her if he wasn't going to be held accountable by God if he divorced her? Not only did he stay with her, but he also remained faithful to her and forgave her. What a man! Was he superman or what? In studying about forgiveness, I realized this man wasn't superman at all. He was loving his wife as Christ loved the church.

The Holy Spirit will help us do things that we couldn't do naturally. The issues that you're dealing with might not be adultery. However, it's big to you. If you are single with a family, you still must forgive. Maybe you went through a situation where the absent parent has not been responsible and left you alone to raise your children. Some of you may have lost a mate by no choice of your own, through death or mental illness, whatever the case may be. They're not here physically or mentally.

Sometimes things we go through will make us angry. You may be angry with God. Whatever the case may be, many of us find ourselves angry with God or questioning Him. You may ask the question "Why me?" As you ask God these questions, you may feel ignored and become angry with God. God can help you forgive God. You read it right. I said God can help you forgive Him. Don't let the enemy make you feel ashamed for being mad at God. Just don't drown in the sea of un-forgiveness. Go to God and tell Him how you feel. If you feel that it's unfair, tell Him. After you get through letting go of how you feel, watch God move on your behalf.

You may not be mad at God. It may be your parents. Maybe they missed the mark in your life. All parents aren't good parents. We don't have to remind them of how bad they are or were as parents. My mom passed away in 2010. Unfortunately, I did get mad at my mom. I called her and told her what a bad parent her and my dad were to me. I remember that day like it was yesterday. Robert and I were paying graduation dues for our middle daughter to graduate. We had three children graduate back to back. Sha was the last one to graduate of our older three children.

I was sitting on the couch one day, and I began to think about when I was the same age as my middle daughter. I was out of school sitting at home with no direction. How could my parents let that happen? The more I thought about it; the more I began to get mad. I was angry with my mother. She was the one who I lived with during my high school years. Why did she let me quit school? I thought about how hard it was for me to get an education after quitting school. Then my heart started beating faster, and I said to myself,

"I'm a parent, and I love my children. I WOULD NEVER LET MY CHILDREN DROP OUT OF SCHOOL."

I picked up the phone and called my mom. She picked up the phone with a sweet voice and said,

"Hi, Felicia."

"Mom, you know what? You and Dad were horrible parents to me. I mean you were horrible. Do you know I just got through paying high school dues for Sha? Robert and I have to work hard to make sure these kids graduate."

I could hear my mom breathing hard, but she let me talk. For a while, there was just silence on the phone. Then I heard her soft voice say,

"I don't know, Felicia. I DON'T KNOW!"

She said she was sorry, and we got off the phone. Now, this happened in June. We spoke to each other every day after this and never brought the subject up again, until May on Mother's Day. Robert and I went to my mom's house to give her a Mother's Day card. When I handed it to her, she looked at it and said,

"I don't think I deserve this, Felicia."

"WHY?" I replied.

"I'm a horrible mother," she said. My heart

just dropped.

"Mom, I'm sorry for what I said about you being a horrible mother. I was just upset. I do wish that you made me finish school. I wish that you had the strength to push and pull me through. I realize that you were fourteen when you got pregnant with me, and fifteen when you had me. It took God to show me that you did the best you could with what you had as a single mother. Now, I'm grown with an education, and you are my number one cheerleader in everything that I do. I love you, Mom. Happy Mother's Day!"

We must forgive our parents no matter what they have done to us in order to move forward in God and in our marriage. If we don't forgive our parents, we will have to deal with it somewhere down the line. When I was growing up, I was a daddy's girl, and I wasn't even around my dad. When I was four-years-old, my dad was no longer around. I searched for him all through my childhood. I found him at the age sixteen, and I found out a lot about him. Some things were uncomfortable. He got my mom pregnant when she was fourteen-years-old, and he was twenty-one. I learned that he was dyslexic, and he couldn't read or write. He could only write his name. In spite of all of this, I just wanted to get to know him. He was my dad. As time went on, my dad ended up in prison for fifteen years. That's a story in itself. It wasn't until I got married that I began to get angry with my dad. I married Robert my best friend. I'm happy that he's always there for me. When I'm down, he always tries to bring me up. I can see how Robert loves and protects me. I started thinking to myself, "Why couldn't my dad do that? Where was he?"

I began to get angry. If it wasn't for strong men in my family, I would have been a lot worse off. I had Uncle James, Uncle Mike, Uncle Eric, and my Great Uncle Robert. My grandfather was also there for me. These were men who meant what they said, and did what they said they were going to do. My Uncle Mike would check on me as far as school, and my Uncle James fed me with the Word of God.

Uncle Eric was tough back then, and he made sure that I didn't take anything for granted when it came to the projects and the street, as far as hanging around the wrong crowd. I realized that my dad had a lot of issues. When he got out of prison, I found him again.

We have lost touch off and on throughout my life. Late one night I was thinking about him, and I decided to call 411 for information.

"Hello, how may I help you? Hello?"

"Yes, is there... I mean, I need the phone number for a Ronald Burke."

"Uh, we have a Ronald L. Burke."

"I believe that's him!"

"You want the number, ma'am?"

"Yes, yes, I do," I replied softly.

It was about 1:00 a.m. I called my dad

anyway.

"Hello, Dad!" I shouted, "dad?"

He shouted, "F E L I C IA! How did you find me girl?"

Our conversation went on and on for hours. He told me that he kept his phone number listed, so I could find him. I wondered, "Why didn't he look for me? What parent waits on their grown child to find them?" I'm not trying to put him down, that is just how I felt at the time.

Believe me forgiveness is indeed a process. I began to share with my husband how I was feeling about my dad. My husband started to not like my dad. He didn't even want me to visit him. The building that he lived in wasn't safe for me to visit, but I went to see him anyway.

I understand that to my husband I am beautiful and deserve the best. When he looked at my dad, he saw a drunk. I began to pray for my dad.

As I prayed for him, I noticed that he had some good traits. He loved to help others.

People took advantage of him because he was always giving. He would be the one that would give someone the shirt right off of his back. I accept my dad just as he is. Although we have lost contact again, because of my love for Christ, I keep looking for him. I hope to find him and lead him to Christ. This is not how God intended for the order of the family to be, but all things work together for the good of them that love the Lord.

My dad might not have been the father he should have been to me, but he still has a chance. Whether he takes it or not; I will still love him, be of service to him, and continue to pray for him. I have forgiven him. This doesn't mean that I don't feel pain sometimes; I've just chosen to give it to God. If I didn't go through the things that I have been through with my Dad, I wouldn't be able to share my experiences with others or show others how to overcome being fatherless.

Forgiveness frees us from hate.
Forgiveness also helps us to be able to trust our husbands and others. If I never forgave my dad, I would be struggling with trust issues. I realize that I am a child of God who has been forgiven by Christ Jesus. Now as a daughter, I offer forgiveness to my father. I trust and believe that God has a plan for my life.

CHAPTER 10

TRUST

Truth is defined as an assured reliance on the character, ability, or strength of someone or something. Someone you trust is one in which confidence is placed, or depending upon something future or contingent. Trust gives hope. We cannot have healthy families without trust.

We need trust for each other. Our children must be able to trust us. If you are a single parent, your children need to trust you. We all need to trust God. Husbands and wives should trust each other. We should create an environment to where we can depend on each other. I need to know I can believe my husband when he says something. My husband must establish trust with me. If he tells me he is going to do something and he can't, he should come to me and explain why. I should be able to believe whatever he tells me. I know Robert's character; he couldn't lie to me without me knowing even if he wanted to. Robert is not a man who practices lying.

If he got away with lying to me, it would change my mind about who I know and believe him to be.

When people practice lying, it is often hard to know whether they're telling the truth or not. If we as adults are accustomed to telling each other lies, how can we trust each other. Lies destroy trust. The truth is what sets us free. No matter how ugly that truth may be. When we lie, we give the devil the tools to use to destroy us. He will come into our home and take full control. We must not mistake uncommunicative conversations for lies. Robert and I have had several miscommunications, and I would say, "Are you lying?"

Now, he hates being called a liar, which I never want to call him a liar; so he will take the time to explain to me what he said or is trying to say. I will listen carefully then tell him what I understood him to be saying. We have learned that different words mean different things to us. I can say, "Alright" in an intense conversation, I mean "Alright", not that I agree with him. Just "Alright,

I'm done talking for now."

His "Alright" means just that, "Alright! Everything is okay", not "Let's talk later." His "Alright" means "OK" to him. He used to think that my "Alright" meant "OK", too.

I should trust him even in the areas that seem like they don't matter much. A matter of an opinion is just an opinion. I understand my husband and I may think different, but I still need to be able to trust the intent of his heart. I know that he wouldn't say or do anything to hurt me intentionally. I said intentionally! Sometimes I can get very emotional and take things too personal.

Our children learn how to trust from us. We teach them to believe us or not to believe us. Sometimes we feel like as parents we don't owe our children any explanation. When we tell them that we are going to do something and we don't, we shouldn't brush things off like we never said it. We need to go to them and let them know we can't do whatever we said we were going to do. Not, "Oh, I said we were going to do that, but whatever, we're not now." When they ask why, we just say, "Because I said so." This is different when our children ask us if they can do something and we say, "No." No means no! They need to learn that as parents we have their best interest at heart. They will learn this over time, but trust is something we teach them at a very young age. Through consistency, we teach our children to trust us by discipline and love.

When our youngest daughter does wrong, she can trust and believe that she will be corrected. If we correct her from some of her wrongdoing and not all, she may lose trust in us. Children lose trust in their parents when there's a lack of consistency. Parents can't be afraid to show love to their children. Some parents read stories to the children every night before they go to bed, tuck them in, and tell them that they love them. The child starts to depend on their parents to tuck them in and read them a story.

When our children are young and we picked them up from school or fixed them dinner, they learned to depend on us. There's a lot of sacrificing when it comes to parenting. I had my first child before the age of twenty. It was very easy for me to run around with my friends and hang out like most young people. Since I had my daughter, I couldn't hang out all day. I had to make sure that she was fed, changed, and clothed. I made sure that my daughter was home for her meals, and that I was with her. When I started work, I would pick her up from daycare and take her home to spend time with her. I would have loved to be with my friends, but I didn't believe in riding my daughter around all day taking her from place to place. She developed a trust and dependence on me. I believe if I had changed our routine and done things differently, her trust in me would have been unstable.

Trust doesn't come over night. Trusting people can be hard. We must be able to display qualities in our family that will allow us to trust each other. Knowing God will help us develop these qualities. Trusting Him should be very easy. We can depend on Him. His Word is true. He always keeps

His promise. His word has never returned to Him void, so why do we have a tough time trusting Him? Maybe it's because we don't feel like we are worthy of God's love. We know we have fallen short in some areas and feel as if God won't be there for us.

The world believes in give-and-take relationships. God is true to His word no matter what. Even when we have fallen short in some areas, He just wants us to trust in His Word. He only denies us what is contrary to His Word. The Bible said that He will withhold no good thing from us.

"For the Lord God is a sun and shield; the Lord bestows favor and honor. No good thing does he withhold from those who walk uprightly" (Psalms 84:11).

Believing and following His Word is trusting in Him. Trusting God is believing He will do what He said He's going to do. If we went against His Word and there were no consequences, wouldn't we begin to distrust Him? Just like children, we earn each other's trust through love. What do we do when that trust is broken? That's a hard question in marriage, and in the family. Trust can be broken when we don't live up to each other's expectations. Is not living up to each other's expectations breaking each other's trust?

It is when we pattern our lives after Christ, but live otherwise. We can't live for Christ and not honor our marriage vows by cheating on our mates. If the Bible tells us that God is a jealous God and marriage is a covenant of God, there's no room for anyone else.

"Thou shalt have no other gods before me. Thou shalt not make unto thee any graven image, or any likeness of anything that is in heaven above, or that is in the earth beneath, or that is in the water under the earth. Thou shalt not bow down thyself to them, nor serve them: for I the Lord thy God am a jealous God, visiting the iniquity of the fathers upon the children unto the third and fourth generation of them that hate me" (Exodus 20:3-5, KJV).

This scripture is not using the word jealous to

mean envious. God wants to be the only Lord in our lives. He won't occupy a space with no one else. He let us know that there are profound consequences for serving other gods. We won't get into all of that.

This chapter is about trust. Right now, we're exploring breaking each other's trust. If someone cheats, has an affair, he or she has broken the marriage covenant. Trust is thrown out the window. The price for this violation is high; the pain is deep. Thank God, we have never experienced this! We know people who have, and the recovery process can be long. Whenever a relationship is broken, the only way to fix it is by rebuilding the trust. Rebuilding starts by being open, telling the truth, and being accountable.

One of my favorite phrases is "Starting at the beginning". Just like we tuck our children into bed each night to reassure them that we love them and will protect them, you should assure your mate that you are committed to them by recommitting yourselves solely and totally to the marriage.

Disconnection from all outsiders that have caused interference in your marriage is key. Admitting to your faults might not be easy, but it must be done in order to rebuild the trust that was once in your marriage. An affair doesn't always have to lead to divorce.

We must work through trust issues in our marriage, just as we have to work on our salvation daily. We shouldn't take our salvation for granted, neither should we take our marriage for granted. As I read more and more of God's Word, the more it makes sense to me why God compares marriage to the church. There have been times in my life where it was hard for me to trust God. I know God wants the best for me, but I haven't always believed that God would give me the best. Why? I didn't think I deserved His best.

The world teaches that we get what we deserve; I'm glad God doesn't operate like that. I have received so much from God that I don't deserve; I'm a sinner saved by grace. When I gave my life to Him, I became royalty just like Him.

When Robert and I bought our house almost three years ago, it was hard for me to trust God through the process. Robert and I had both messed up our credit. We needed good credit to buy our house, so we worked on building our credit up. I had a hard time forgiving myself for ruining my credit. I cried out to the Lord daily and told Him how sorry I was. I believed that God would honor my heart and direct Robert and I in finding a good house. However, I waivered back and forth between what I deserved in the natural from my own actions, and what God had for me. I had trust in the Lord, but I also had some doubt because of my own actions. I was trying to figure things out and make sense of things that were unclear.

"Trust in the Lord with all your heart and lean not on your own understanding; in all your ways submit to him, and he will make your paths straight" (Proverbs 3:5-6, NIV). It has become so easy for me to trust God now, because I know I can't lean on my own understanding. I don't go by whether things make sense or not. My faith is strong; I will tell my friends and family that God will withhold no good things from me. That's why I don't get caught up in material things. I know if I want something and my heart is right, God will give it to me. Believe it or not; I don't even have to have the money for it either!

"For the LORD God is a sun and shield: the LORD will give grace and glory: no good thing will he withhold from them that walk uprightly" (Psalms 84:11, KJV).

"Behold, I will do a new thing; now it shall spring forth; shall ye not know it? I will even make a way in the wilderness, and rivers in the desert" (Isaiah 43:19, KJV).

"Take delight in the LORD, and he will give you the desires of your heart" (Psalms 37:4, NIV).

I trust God because He has never failed me. Anything that I have earnestly sought after in His will, He has given to me. Material things will fade away, cars will break down, houses need repaired, but God's Word will always last.

Every word of God is flawless; he is a shield to those who take refuge in him" (Proverbs 30:5)

"Anyone who believes in him will never be put to shame" (Romans 10:11, NIV).

"Dear friends, if our hearts do not condemn us, we have confidence before God and receive from him anything we ask, because we keep his commands and do what pleases him" (I John 3:21-22, NIV).

I share these scriptures with you to build up your trust in God. I know when you get through reading this book; you will be full of the Word.

There are still times when I go through challenges and wonder why God loves the imperfect me so much? It's because He has looked beyond my faults, and supplied all my needs.

CHAPTER 11

RESPECT

Respect is treating each other right no matter how we feel, what we think, or what we want to do in the moment. We can't possibly love each other without respecting each other. Treating each other right is an easy way to define respect.

I have found out that the meaning of respect is different from culture to culture. I have friends from all over the world. We may have different opinions on what is defined as disrespect, but most of us do agree on what respect is in general. It is very important for single people to find out what his or her own values are before getting married. Some men and women weren't raise in the same way. I came from a family where it wasn't disrespectful for a woman to give her opinion to her husband. I was taught that women should handle themselves with decency, no room for arguing with her husband in public or in front of others. Men would also respect their wives in public and behind closed doors. There should be no worries of "Wait until I see you later". God does not agree with any type of abuse!

A man who puts his hands on a woman to harm her and control her is out of the will of God. This is a true form of disrespect. Sometimes it's hard for different cultures to decide whose way is right, their cultural beliefs or God's way. God's way is always right. The Word teaches us that there is a way that seems right to man, but no good comes from it.

"There is a way which seemeth right unto a man, but the end thereof are the ways of death" (Proverbs 14:12).

When we ask God to be the ruler over our lives, we need to give Him full reign over our cultural beliefs as well.

Taking a stand for our family is necessary if we want the blessings of God. Disrespect in the form of abuse not only comes from men abusing women but also from women abusing men; it can be verbal, physical, or even emotional abuse.

I did a good job at this when I was in my twenties. I was so afraid of being with someone who would abuse and misuse me, so I became the abuser. I did some things right and a lot of things wrong. I abused other men emotionally, physically, and verbally. I was determined that my children would have a good father in their lives. I believed in the principles of God, but in this area, I wasn't practicing them. If you asked me, I had a right to be controlling. I learned that it was so easy for me to create a mess and ask God to clean it up.

If I had waited for my husband a long time ago, I would have saved myself from a lot of headaches. God had to take me down a long road to redemption to learn His plan for my life and my children. Once I accepted His plan for my life, I began to have a love for Christ like never before. I'm glad I learned true respect before I got married. I don't think it was the fact that I never knew what respect was, but I allowed myself to get into unhealthy relationships before I got married, which caused me to be out of order.

Thank God, I came from a family where there are great leaders, so I had a good foundation to draw from. My uncle, Bishop James, showed our family how men should love and respect women. My uncle and Aunt Mary kind of remind me of myself and Robert. Uncle James is a quiet laid-back man. Until he gets in the pulpit to preach, then he's a whole different person. Every time he preaches, I know God is real! God can take a quiet man and have him preach the gospel, yell, jump, and shout. "He's a great God!

My aunt Mary on the other hand is, the opposite. She has no problem with speaking her mind, right or wrong, she will let others know how she feels, and then beg their pardon later.

Robert is quiet and laid back like my uncle; now, I told you in previous chapters that he came from a family that loved to curse. He's saved by grace now and is a changed man. Me on the other hand, I'm like my aunt in some ways. I will speak what's on my mind. I'm just a little more reserved;

but if I'm challenging something or someone, it must be serious. Over all, my husband and I are both peaceful people. We share the same values of respect. We are now drawing from the same well, Jesus Christ.

Our children learn how to respect others from us. My daughters are learning from me how to respect men by how I treat Robert. Most of the time, they don't even know when we're having a disagreement. Sometimes, I will let them know when I'm upset, because they need to see how I treat my husband when I'm upset with him. I don't try to make him miserable, by not taking care of his needs. I still do the same things for him as always. I think when we're not getting along we are just miserable ourselves. We just want to be in each other's good graces. That's how we should feel about God. It shouldn't be so easy for us to go against His will. It should tear us up inside when we're going against His principles. The world says get even when you're mad, but God teaches us to love.

"Beloved, let us love one another: for love is of God; and everyone that loveth is born of God, and knoweth God" (1 John 4:7, KJV).

It's hard to still do things for each other when we're upset. I could tell Robert to make his own dinner. He could decide not to pay the bills or answer my calls, just because we don't agree sometimes.

We still have a home to run. If I didn't respect Robert, it would start a chain reaction. No one in the house would respect him. Our youngest daughter certainly wouldn't know what to expect from her husband when she gets married. If Robert didn't respect me, I'm sure she would try to run over me. Following the chain of command helps keep our family on track. Children don't respect adults who don't respect each other. No respect in the home leads to disrespect outside of the home. Disrespect outside of the home shows no home training. Let's get our priorities right in our homes, so we can raise good leaders. Our children are the communities of the future. No one's family is perfect; we will all get upset with each other as well as our children. We are a team; we keep it moving in spite of the challenges that may come our way. We just move with respect and love.

CHAPTER 12

INVADERS

"To thrust or force in or upon someone or something especially without permission, welcome, or fitness."

Don't allow invaders to come into your family. Invaders come to intrude and destroy the foundation that you have built your family upon. Your children will see the opposite of what you are teaching them in school and on TV. Those things most families are already on the lookout for. It's the things that we have become comfortable with that ease in and invade our children's thought patterns. We still need to have conversations with our children to see what they are being taught in school as well as Sunday school. When they come home from school, we should be finding out what their lessons were about that day.

Nowadays, children are learning about sex education in school, without any opinions or discussions with the parents. This leaves room for our children to take it as a fact whatever they learn at school about sex education. Those of us that don't have a problem teaching sex education to our children at home have set a foundation for them. We have taught our children to wait until marriage to have sex. We try to teach them that God meant for sex to be enjoyed between a husband and wife. I say a husband and wife, because we have taught them that marriage is between a man and a woman.

There are many people today, who oppose what the Bible teaches. The focus is more on marriage being for a man and woman, but the Bible also speaks of not coveting our neighbor's spouse and so much more. The school system teaches more about disease and protection; I guess because so many young people are getting sexually transmitted diseases at young ages along with numerous teenage pregnancies.

It's hard to keep our children on track when most of their classmates are having sex. Sometimes they know the principles but still make the wrong choices. I remember when my grandmother found out that I was pregnant. Wow! First, she asked how many times I did it! I was shocked and surprised! I felt it was none of her business to be asking me such questions; however, she had every right to ask me whatever she wanted to. She did a good job in helping my mom raise me, but she never told me why I should wait until I got married. She just said don't do it.

Well, I try to tell my children why they should wait until they get married. Not just because they can get pregnant or get a disease, but I also let them know that they should not give their bodies to anyone that they are not willing to give their hearts to in marriage. That one should be the one that God has chosen for them. I let them know that girls and boys will like each other. They will turn into young adults who like each other. It's ok to like the opposite sex. It's quite natural to start to have feelings for one another. It's knowing what to do with those feelings. Knowing how to date in groups, so they won't be left alone to try to experiment. We have to have these tough conversations, or their minds will be invaded!

They will believe what they are taught in some schools. For example, some say that it is ok to practice masturbation. There are no clear scriptures to say that the act of masturbation is a sin. Think of it this way though. If we allow our children to think that it's ok, we are teaching them it's ok to please our flesh and to give in to our desires. Now, the Bible does clearly speak against this. These are things that our children face, not just our children but adults too!

We must learn how to discuss difficult things with our children and each other. If we don't know the answers, then we need to pray about it and tell them we will have to discuss it later. Don't take too long to get back with them. Most children think that their parents are old and crazy, and don't know what they're talking about. We still owe it to them to raise them in the right way by the Word of God.

Our family values can be invaded in many

ways. If you are single and trying to do the right thing, it will be hard. The enemy will try to tell you that you don't have to live alone, and that it's ok to live with someone or create a mother or father for your children. People are doing just that. Some even feel like they have waited on God long enough. Some have even decided to go to a sperm bank to conceive and have children. You may have had friends who have chosen one of those routes. They may seem to have a great family, but that's not the way God intended for the family to be formed.

When we open the door, and invite intruders or invaders in, they are no longer intruders or invaders. They are your guests, and you are giving them permission and access to your life. When we allow immoral things to dictate how we live our lives, we cannot expect God to be in control. We must first get rid of the intruders or invaders. Let every thought and every action be subject to the will of God. Anything that's not, let it be known as an invader or intruder. When we recognize that we have unwelcome guests, we can command them to leave.

When we live a double standard, we must choose one standard and invite God in. We cannot get mad if God is not in control of our lives, if we haven't invited Him in. Not just for a visit, but He also needs to take control over our lives.

I can always spot the spirit of invasion when it comes to marriage and family. I love to correct people when they say that there are "No good men left". When I hear that, I'm always quick to respond.

"Yes, there are a lot of good men in the world. I know a lot of them myself. My son is a good man, my uncles, and brother-in-law's. I have neighbors who are good men."

Then, I'll suggest that they do something different and hang around different people, and maybe they will see some good men. I will not give into negativity.

People love to voice their opinions about things, and they love to intrude and destroy other's family values. Some people will say all men are into pornography, even Christian men. I say "No, nope", and if all the men you know are involved in those type of things, then maybe you need some new friends. I know that most men will come across some pornography. If it's a Jet magazine, a Victoria's Secret book, or a swim suit magazine, they will come across some form of pornography. That doesn't mean that they will practice pornography.

I know there was a gospel-recording artist that admitted to being addicted to pornography. He gave it to God and was delivered from that addiction. That's just one man! Yes, it is a big thing, but not every man is addicted to pornography. We cannot let people lead us to believe the things that we know are wrong. Just like with masturbation, no scriptures say that pornography is a sin. There are scriptures that are clear when it comes to the flesh. Just because it doesn't come out and say masturbation or pornography is wrong, doesn't mean that it isn't wrong.

Just do the test yourself, maybe you're not a

Christian. Anything you must hide and do is wrong. Anything you don't want your children to see you do is wrong. I know some of you may say, "It's not wrong to have sex with my spouse". Yes, that's right, but it is wrong to have sex in front of your children or someone else. Pornography is either watching someone have sex or looking at someone naked in a magazine or by way of television, or whatever technology you may use. People who are exposed in a sexual way or something you look at in a sexual way is a form of pornography. I have added some scriptures for you to read in your spare time. They are written here, but there's much more to it. I would suggest reading the whole chapter.

"For men shall be lovers of their own selves, covetous, boasters, proud, blasphemers, disobedient to parents, unthankful, unholy…"

(2 Timothy 3:2, KJV).

"Do you not know that your body is a temple of the Holy Spirit within you, whom you have from God? You are not your own, 20 for you were bought with a price. So glorify God in your body" (1

Corinthians 6:19-20, ESV).

"For everything in the world—the lust of the flesh, the lust of the eyes, and the pride of life—comes not from the Father but from the world" (1 John 2:16, NIV).

"You will have these tassels to look at and so you will remember all the commands of the Lord, that you may obey them and not prostitute yourselves by chasing after the lusts of your own hearts and eyes" (Numbers 15:39, NIV).

The enemy will invade our minds with thoughts, people's opinions, and even our own opinions. People now may say it's ok for Christians to drink, if they don't get drunk. I wonder who draws the line. Should I drink enough to get tipsy or come close to being drunk, but not quite drunk? What's the meaning of Christians drinking? Is it to feel good, or get pumped up to dance or what? These are the questions I ask myself. No, it's not a sin to drink. Some people say they only drink a glass of wine with dinner. After all, a little wine is good for the stomach's sake. I have heard it all! New Year's is a good time to have a drink too.

I was taught not to drink at all if I wanted to live a Christian life. Now, I have heard of many Christian people drinking and actually have seen some for myself. I'm not in their houses. I don't know how often they drink, or if they get drunk or not. I like when my husband and I go places and people are drinking, and they ask us why we aren't drinking. Like when we go on cruises, we tell them that we are Christians, and we don't drink. People will look so amazed. I have had people ask me how we can dance with no alcohol in our systems. I will tell them that I have enough joy on my own; I can dance all night. Since it's hard for me to determine how much liquor a Christian should consume and still be a Christian without being drunk, I just don't drink. I know that I'm an evangelist, elder, or minister in the works; I sustain from strong drinks. The Bible teaches that those in leadership should stay away from strong drinks. I must say people will try anything to get folks to drink. Robert and I love to have clean fun. We like to dance and go to comedy shows. We just love going places together.

Now, when we go to comedy shows I love to order virgin strawberry daiquiris. I thought that meant no alcohol. Once we went to see a Gary

Owens show, and I ordered a daiquiri. As I was drinking it, I looked at Robert.

"Robert, this has alcohol in it."

"It's a virgin daiquiri," he replied.

"Yes, but it tastes like there is alcohol in it."

"Well, don't drink it."

I had already drunk most of it.

Since I don't drink, it doesn't take much to get me tipsy. I always joke with Robert and say that we will have a toast on our anniversary. That never happens; we use sparkling cider. I don't think it would be a sin to have a toast with real alcohol; it's just hard to know where to draw the line. I come from an apostolic background. When in doubt, just don't do it. If it convicts you, don't do it.

"And do not be drunk with wine, in which is dissipation; but be filled with the Spirit" (Ephesians 5:18).

Things creep into our lives when we decide to lower our standards for our family. If you have no standards at all, then your family will become the devil's playground. Don't allow others to bypass your standards! Normally, when I order a virgin strawberry daiquiri, it's just that, a pure strawberry daiquiri without alcohol!

CHAPTER 13

DELIVERANCE

"Being freed from any stronghold that has had our family in bondage through thoughts, words, or actions."

Our minds are very powerful. Through our minds, we believe and think things that just aren't true. Wives, we must not let the enemy whisper in our ears that our husbands don't love us. "He doesn't spend time with me" or "He doesn't love me like he used to" are both lies from the pit of hell. One thought leads to another and another. Before you know it, you will be the one distancing yourself from your husband. Husbands don't allow the enemy to tell you that your wives are disrespectful. When you believe that your wife is disrespectful, you will begin to disregard her feelings. If a husband feels like his wife doesn't respect him, it's hard for him to show love towards her. Women shouldn't allow the enemy to tell them that their husbands don't deserve to be respected. We should respect each other no matter what, no matter what we feel the person deserves. When we do what God commands us to do no matter what we think or feel, He will bring deliverance.

"You will not have to fight this battle. Take up your positions; stand firm and see the **deliverance** the LORD will give you, O Judah and Jerusalem" (2 Chronicles 20:17, NIV).

God will deliver us of all strongholds!

Single parents, never let the enemy tell you that you will never get married. Don't let people speak words of untruth into your life either. When I was single, I never entertained the thought that I would ever get married. Until one day, Robert, who was my friend at the time, spoke about marriage. He said, "Um, let me see. One, two, three, four, that's a lot of kids."

Robert, who is very outspoken, was thinking and sharing his thoughts aloud. At the time, he was wondering and thinking, "Can I take care of her and these children like they need to be taken care of?"

I said, "What!?!"

From then on, I said, "This man is crazy, and he doesn't have any children of his own. No, that's not my husband." I listened to the enemy. I told God, "Oh well, if I'm not married by the age of thirty-five, I won't be getting married."

God probably looked down from heaven, smiled, and said, "Yeah right!"

I got married three months before my thirty-sixth birthday. God can be humorous. I had to be delivered first from my thoughts, words, and actions. I had to be delivered from believing the lies I told myself, the lies the enemy told me, and the lies that others may have said.

Yes, Robert and I have four children that we have raised together. The youngest was six when we got married. The other three were in their early teens. We don't have any children together, but we love each other just the same. We realize children don't make our marriage, but they are our gifts from God. As long as we have each other, we are blessed. Robert says that he has been blessed with a family designed by God. We love to share our story because it shows the power of God.

Whether you are a single parent or married, we need deliverance in order to be what God wants us to be in our family. Sometimes we need to be delivered from our actions. I know you've heard that actions speak louder than words. Choosing to not act or behave, as we should, can lead to a lot of trouble in the home. This includes doing things to purposely get on each other's nerves, acting as if we don't care about each other, and choosing not to serve each other by not doing what makes each other happy. We need to be delivered from selfishness, you know the "Me" syndrome of what we want, need and feel.

We also need to help our children become delivered from their thoughts, words, and actions.

The enemy will try to get into our children's minds, by making them think that their friends know more than their parents do or that their parents are old fashioned and don't know what they're talking about. Everyone is doing whatever he wants them to do. The only way our children can be delivered from the enemy tying to destroying their family values is to know the voice of the Lord and the enemy. When we teach our children to use these tools, they can resist the enemy, and he will flee from them.

"Submit yourselves, then, to God. Resist the devil, and he will flee from you" (James 4:7, NIV).

My children were young when they were taught the importance of knowing the voice of the Lord. I had to teach them that knowing I wouldn't always be around to protect them. Knowing God's voice is more than an instinct. Our instinct will kick in when we sense that something is wrong. God will warn us, even when there seems to be nothing wrong. The Word says that we his children know his voice.

"My sheep hear my voice, and I know them, and they follow me" (John 12:27, NIV),

I studied the word with them and asked them to tell me how they knew the voice of the Lord. I asked them if His voice was loud or soft, powerful or gentle. Many times, they just listened to me and responded by saying, "I don't know," which seemed to be the favorite phrase of their generation.

As they began to grow up, they would tell me stories and give me examples of knowing the Lord's voice. I can remember one of the children saying, "Mom, His voice sounded something like mine, just in my head."

I laughed! See, we all have a conscious, an ability to know when something is wrong. The Lord will speak to His children though. I told my children His voice might sound like it's in your head. I said to them,

"One way you can know the voice of the Lord is when He gives you clear instruction on something that's good to keep you from danger, something you know you wouldn't tell yourselves to do, or not do."

The Lord won't appear to be good, but lead you to destruction. I know when I was growing up, sometimes it was hard for me to know the difference between the Lord's voice and my own will. I remember one day that I was walking home from work. I was about fourteen-years-old, and the spirit of the Lord told me to go a different way home than I normally would go. I wrestled with myself trying to figure out if it was my mind or the Lord telling me this. Well, I decided to take the route home that I had always taken.

The route I took barely had any sidewalks to walk on. I always had to walk over an overpass; but as soon as I got over the overpass, my aunt's house was right there. I walked down the street over the overpass to my aunt's house. As soon as I got close to her house, a car sped up out of nowhere. All I needed to do was turn to my right, and I would have been home. Suddenly, the car pulled diagonally in front of me. I looked up, and there was a man staring at me. I began to pray to myself, "Lord Jesus, I should have gone the other way. Jesus," I said and looked the man straight in the eye. As I walked around the car, he drove off.

I learned that it was the spirit of the Lord telling me to go the other way. My Grandma taught me to know the voice of the Lord, so I taught my children to know the voice of the Lord and follow His guidance. I also taught them how important words are and never let anyone speak a negative word over their lives. I remember when I was a teenager, an adult who was angry at the world spoke to me. She said that my best friend, my cousin, and I would all grow up to have men that would beat us. My Lord, when she spoke that word to us, my cousin started to cry. She couldn't believe this woman was saying such things. I grabbed her by the hand at about sixteen-years-old, and I said, "Listen, that's just the devil. We will not grow up to have men who will beat us." God is great! We never have had men in our lives who were abusers.

Our children need to be delivered from wrong choices and straying away from the values we taught them by the Word of the Lord. They can't let bad choices destroy their whole lives. We all need to be restored back to the way God wants us to be. You may not have had Biblical principles in your home growing up. You need to free yourselves from believing that it's too late for you and your family. Don't allow the devil to keep you in strongholds. Strong holds will cripple you and your family. Strongholds come when we refuse to hear and obey God.

The enemy will use the same game, line, and trick that he has used on other members of your family to get a hold of you. If your dad was an alcoholic, he will try to get you addicted to alcohol and drugs. Remember same tricks same game. He'll use addiction or other things to get you such as drugs, sex, and a false sense of love. Some men will lust and misuse women only to get what they want cheap thrill. There are so many women falling for a sense of false love, just wanting to be loved.

If you are in any stronghold, ask for deliverance. God will deliver you. He will teach you His voice to help you stay away from all evil.

CHAPTER 14

WILL GOD BLESS A FAMILY THAT

DOESN'T ACKNOWLEDGE HIM

He that doesn't honor God will fail. Remember the story of the three little pigs. A house built without a solid foundation will come crashing down. The enemy won't even have to huff and puff hard, all he'll have to do is blow a little. On Christ the solid rock we stand. All other grounds are sinking sand. The enemy comes to steal, kill, and destroy. He will make it look like a household without God is blessed. Don't believe your eyes. He's a liar! Some will have gold and riches in this life, but I'd rather have Jesus more than anything.

The blessing of the Lord is full and plenty. Have you ever heard of the candy Now and Later? I'd rather have my blessings now and later. I can receive blessings here on earth, as well as in heaven. Be not deceived, God cannot lie. His Word says that His wish for us is that we prosper, even as our soul shall prosper. That tells me that I will be blessed here on earth as well as in heaven. We must keep our eyes on Christ. I know sometimes that the world seems to be living it up. They are surely eating and drinking! Tomorrow, they will die and be delivered to the God of this world. Life will be over as they know it. There will be no more blessings for them after living a life full of sin.

There are no true blessings without God! Never has been, and never will be! The fool has said in his heart that there is no God.

"The fool has said in his heart, there is no God. They are corrupt, they have done abominable works, there is none that does good" (Psalm 14:1).

See, it is foolish not to let God rule and rain supreme in our home, in our lives.

"God sets the solitary in families: he brings out those who are bound with chains: but the rebellious dwell in a dry land" (Psalms 68:6).

We want to be blessed and not to remain in dry

lands. How can God set a solid foundation in our homes if we don't allow Him to?

"The blessing of the Lord, it maketh rich, and he addeth no sorrow with it" (Proverbs 10:22).

What a great God we serve! He gives to us freely without any sorrow. I wonder. Do we give to each other the same way He gives to us? I know some of us don't. The Bible says give and it shall be given to you.

"Give and it shall be given unto you; good measure, pressed down, and shaken together and running over will be put into your bosom. For with the same measure that you use, it will be measured back to you" (Luke 6:38, NKJV).

If we give to others with a good heart, surely God will take care of us. He takes care of His own, those who love and obey Him. It's very hard to acknowledge someone that you don't even know, or receive blessings from some unknown being. Many people won't accept gifts from a stranger in fear of owing them. Some of us would even ask the question, "What do you, the Giver, want from me?" I'm not telling you to accept any gifts from a stranger. If you have never asked God to be your Lord and Savior, He is indeed a stranger to you.

"Ask, and it shall be given you; seek, and ye shall find; knock, and it shall be opened unto you" (Matthew 7:7, KJV).

All you have to do is seek Him through His Word and through prayer. He will make Himself known to you. Let Him be Lord of your life. Once you get to know Him, it's hard to deny Him!

Jesus Christ is the best gift I have ever and will ever receive. I grew up going to church. I was ten years old when I received the Holy Spirit. I went to the church that my grandmother took me to, which was an apostolic church. I studied the Word continuously throughout my youth. I have believed in Jesus all my life, but why? Why did I go to an apostolic church? I knew as a child that I couldn't make it into heaven holding on to my grandmother's coat tail.

Jesus taught love not hate. Why did Jesus die for my sins? He did it just for me! I realize the apostolic church taught the doctrine of the apostles from the Day of Pentecost. I appreciate my upbringing and my foundation. Now, I go to a non-denominational church. We simply believe in Lord Jesus Christ and the Bible to be true. I believe in the doctrine of Christ. I believe that God is no respect of persons. In order to be His children, we must allow Him to be our Father. You must know Him for yourself!

There's a song we used to sing in church, "Pass me not, oh gentle Savior. Do not pass me by. I'm asking you Savior, oh, ooh, Savior, while on others thou are calling. Do not pass me by."

God can't bless a house that refuses to acknowledge Him, because He is the blessing Himself. When we have Him, He will flow through our house like a river of living water. He will supply all our needs.

"But God shall supply all your need according to his riches in glory by Christ Jesus" (Philippians 4:1).

"That you may be children of your Father in heaven. He causes his sun to rise on the evil and the good, and sends rain on the righteous and the unrighteous" (Mathew 5:45).

Remember God rains on evil and good, but he doesn't bless that which is evil. If your family has chosen not to acknowledge God, they will still feel the overflow of His love, but not His blessings.

"He replied, 'Blessed rather are those who hear the word of God and obey it'" (Luke 11:28, NIV).

"Then Jesus told him, 'Because you have seen me, you have believed; blessed are those who have not seen and yet have believed'" (John 20:29, NIV).

Don't be fooled by how things may appear; having riches doesn't mean you are blessed. Good health and material things are part of blessings. True blessing comes from living for Jesus Christ.

CHAPTER 15

FAITH

Faith is relying on God no matter what the situation looks like and believing in His word no matter what. Faith means knowing that God will not withhold any good thing from us.

Sometimes we go through pressures in life. These pressures may cause us to cry, want to scream, and literally bring us to our knees. Crying is a form of release and also a form of cleansing. Because we may display some discomfort on the outside, doesn't mean that we don't have faith. It's when we stop moving in faith that it hurts us. We must show some action by praying and declaring God's Word to Him. We can start by saying, "Lord your Word says".

Faith is anticipating, waiting, looking for, and expecting God to move no matter what the circumstance look like. Losing faith is when we stop and quit moving forward towards what God has promised us. We must keep a positive attitude. The devil would have us to believe things are a lot worse than what they seem to be. We seem to go by what we see. If it looks bad, we tend to believe things are bad.

Robert and I have been looking for a house for about two years. Well, not actually going out looking, but going through a list of houses on the internet and getting an idea of what we want. Then, the day finally came when it was time for us to go out looking for a house. I was so excited! I love looking at houses. We even thought about getting our house built, so we went to talk to a contractor. Most of the plans we saw, we didn't like. We decided to go with a house that was already built, not too new and not too old. This house had a living room, dining room, basement, family room, four bathrooms, master suite, two-car garage, and a privacy-fenced backyard. There was also cathedral ceilings; even an open walk-in closet, whirlpool tub, loft, and open kitchen! Man, we both loved this house. It was a short sale in a suburban area. Wow! I thought, "This is our house!"

We put in a bid; the bid was over the amount that the seller was asking for. We received a counter offer, and that's when things started to look ugly. The seller saw that we had bid over the amount, so they wanted us to pay their seller fees, utilities fee, and you name it. I said that we liked the house, but we were not going to jump through hoops to get to it. "We'll keep looking," I said to our broker.

I remembered awhile back that a preacher had prophesied that God would give me a house built from the ground up, if I wanted it. He said if you want five bedrooms and four bathrooms, God will give it to you. This was a real word from the Lord. This pastor didn't know me. He certainly didn't know that I had lost a five-bedroom, four-bathroom home.

As my broker and I went to look for houses, I reflected on what this pastor prophesied about thirteen years ago. I prayed to myself and said, "Lord, we are not asking for five bedrooms or four bathrooms. We just want four bedrooms and two and a half baths. That's all we need. Lord, I know you will supply all of our needs and give us more than enough with much overflow. Lord, our hearts are in the right place. We know if you can bless us with a five-bedroom, four-bathroom home, surely you will give us what we need and are asking for."

Every week, for about a month, we went to look for houses. I began to get sad. Every house was either a short sale or foreclosure. Short sales are a long process. I prayed for the people who were losing their homes. We wanted God to bless us with a deal, but not at someone else's expense. After looking for a month, we found a house.

I knew it was our house as soon as I walked in. When I went upstairs, I noticed that one of the bedrooms was painted half-pink and half-blue. This room had a vertical line separating the two colors. At our current house, our daughters painted their room pink and blue. With a horizontal line separating the two colors. I said to myself, "Yes, Lord, this is a sign. This is our house." The broker then told us that this house was also a short sale. My face dropped. The broker said we could put in a bid, but we may not hear anything for a while.

Robert then looked at her and said, I'm willing to wait.

I smiled, "Really? Sweet!"

"Yes!"

I looked at the broker and said, "Yep, we'll wait."

We put in a bid for a little bit more than what they were asking for. We got a response back from the first lender two weeks later. Yes, I said the FIRST lender. We didn't hear from the second lender until two months later.

We have had a long process. We are still going through the buying process, but we have gotten extensions. The enemy has even whispered to me, "This is not your house."

The Lord just told me to keep on packing. As our move-out date keeps changing, I keep packing. Sometimes, I'm hard headed, and my attitude stinks. I ask for forgiveness, but I keep on moving towards the promise that God has for us.

I choose to share that story because I want you to know that sometimes we do experience pain while having faith. The enemy will put pressure on us to cause us to be uncomfortable and want to give up. He will create a dark picture, so we won't see the light at the end of the tunnel. Some days, I have cried working through the challenges before me. I would be lying if I said I never felt like giving up. It's so easy to quit. We show strength when we fight for what God has for us. The Bible tells us to fight the good fight of faith.

"Fight the good fight of faith, lay hold on eternal life, to which you are also called, and have professed a good profession before many witnesses" (1 Timothy 6:12).

We fight to have eternal life in Jesus Christ. We also fight for what we have inherited in this life. God loves and takes care of His children.

A while ago, our son had gotten into a relationship with a girl who was nothing but trouble. She was an up and coming gold digger. She had been taught by her mom to get all she could from a man. When Robert and I met, this girl named Chereta, we thought she was a nice Christian girl. Her father didn't live in the home with her, but he was a deacon. Chereta would talk about how much she loved the Lord. She was always involved in church activities. In fact, her and my son went to Bible study together for the church, summer, and winter camp meeting. They were doing many positive things together that most kids their age wouldn't think about being involved in. Robert and I were so proud of our son for having a Christian girlfriend.

Chereta also went to school with our daughter Sha. Sha and Chereta graduated on the same day. This was a heartfelt event, and Chereta was full of tears when she accepted her diploma. She had been very sick the whole year. Her mother didn't know if she would live to graduate.

One day, Chereta had spent the night at her dad's house. She had been feeling strange most of the day, but didn't know why. She went into the bathroom. She began to feel faint as she sat down on the toilet. Tom, Chereta's dad, saw her go into the bathroom. An hour had passed. When he didn't see Chereta come out of the bathroom, he knocked on the door.

"Chereta, Chereta, Chereta!"

He shouted loud and fast. His heart began to race.

"Chereta! Chereta!"

Tom banged on the door and pushed his body up against it. The door was locked. As he panicked, he walked away from the door. Then with little space to gather speed, he ran toward the door with full speed. Tom took a deep breath, and he kicked the door in. There lay his daughter on the floor.

"Ohhhhhhhhhhhhhh! God!"

Tom's word slurred as if he were a drunkard.

"Please, God!"

He got down on the bathroom floor by his daughter. He shook her and shook her. There was no response, but she was breathing.

"Hold on, baby."

He ran, got a phone, and dialed 911.

"911," a soft voice answered.

"I need an ambulance now!"

"Sir, what's the problem?"

"My daughter is passed out on the bathroom floor."

"Has she taken any drugs?"

"DRUGS? DRUGS! This is my daughter for the love of GOD! GET SOMEONE OUT HERE!"

"Sir, they are on their way. Please don't hang up! Stay on the line. How old is your Daughter?"

"She is seventeen. They are here."

"Okay, good luck sir!"

The paramedics put Chereta on the stretcher, with Tom close by her side. When they arrived at the hospital, Chereta was unconscious. Doctors and nurses rushed to see why Chereta was unconscious, and they began to ask questions.

"Are you sure your daughter is not on any medication? Did you see any pill bottles in the bathroom? Has your daughter ever been on drugs?

Tom shouted, "No, no, no medication! No drugs! Let's stop wasting time. Please, can you find out what happened to my daughter?"

As they wheeled Chereta to a room, the nurse gently pulled Tim to the side. She began to talk softly.

OK sir, I know you're upset. Please understand that these are the questions that we need to ask you. We are trying hard to get to the bottom of this. I'm sure your daughter will be okay. At least for now, she is breathing although she's unresponsive. Her respiration seems to be okay, so let's hope for the best."

Eventually, Chereta did come around. She had to go through intense therapy and speech with still no exact diagnosis as to what happened or what caused her to pass out and be unresponsive the day her dad found her in the bathroom. As everyone watched Chereta, she reached for her diploma with tears in her eyes thinking about what happened on the day that she passed out in the bathroom. Everyone's eyes were filled with tears because they knew that if it wasn't for God, Chereta would not have made it to see her graduation. What a day to celebrate as Chereta walked down the aisle, she held her diploma in her hand and waved it high.

Chereta had told me about what happened the day she passed out at her dad's house while she was in the bathroom. Even though her and James hadn't been together that long, I couldn't help but reflect on the story that she had told me. When I saw her waving her diploma in the air, I too had tears in my eyes. I began to yell, "GO CHERETA!"

After graduation, my daughter Sha had a graduation party. Chereta was there and everything seemed to be fine. Chereta seemed to be a part of our family. Every event we had, my son would invite her. One day, my daughter decided to have a party for my granddaughter at the park. Her birthday is in September, so it wasn't necessarily hot or cold. The weather was somewhat windy, but everyone still enjoyed himself or herself. The adults were around to help the children play as they rode on their bikes, swung on the swings, and ran around the playground area. When Chereta and James arrived at the party, it seemed like everything stopped. Chereta had on some tight, tight shorts with a shirt that barely covered her stomach. As they walked up to the park, Chereta had her hands all over my son. There was music playing, and I don't know where the music was coming from. Chereta heard the music, turned around, and backed her behind towards my son. She said, "Oh, that's my song," as she began to shake her backside all over my son's private parts. I was so embarrassed, and everyone in the family was looking with their eyes big like "What is Chereta doing?" My son began to walk away towards the people.

From that day on, Chereta began to show her true colors. This girl, who appeared to be very sickly and a nice Christian young woman, started to see my son as an ATM machine. She would call our house to speak to James and ask him to bring her food, deodorant, or you name it. At first, I did feel uncomfortable like what she was doing wasn't right, but they were young. Young people do many things that their parents do not necessarily agree with, and they must learn by their own experiences. I knew that we had to talk to our son. We also had to trust his judgment; but as time went on, the relationship which seemed to have made my son very happy became a nightmare. Chereta would continue to call James for money. She called him and told him that her mom had went to a fast food restaurant and brought her sister something, but she didn't bring her anything. When she asked her mom where her food was, her mom replied, "Call your boyfriend!

James became very upset and began to voice his opinion very strongly over the phone. When he told me, what was going on, I told him she was a gold digger.

"Mom, Mom, how could she be a gold digger when I don't even have money like that?"

I explained it to him.

"To you, you don't have anything; Chereta, she sees a young man who is a good guy that goes to work every day, doesn't get into trouble, and basically is a clean-cut type of guy. She knows that you love her and will do anything for her. Don't get me wrong, she is your girlfriend. As your girlfriend, you will do anything for her. When a girl changes her focus from you to what you have and what you can give her, there is problem. When her mom keeps telling her to call you for everything, there's a problem. You cannot let people take your kindness for weakness. Remember, you are not her husband. You guys are young, and you are just dating her."

As time went on, Robert and I began to learn that the way Sherry, Chereta's mother, was living was the way she was training Chereta to live. She, too, had men supplying her every need. My son was so wrapped up in Chereta; he couldn't see that she was bad news for him. She would have other guys coming to her house and my son to her house too. When my son would arrive at her house and either see another guy leaving or sitting in the car, he asked Chereta,

"Who is that guy sitting in the car?"

"I don't know. It's some guy that's been bothering me, an ex-boyfriend."

In fact, Chereta was playing games with these guys. Whichever one would bring her what she wanted is who she would call. If more than one guy arrived at the same time, then she would play like she didn't know what was going on.

Robert and I began to pray for James. We would pray that God would give James the strength to see Chereta for who she really was. God may not come when we want Him, but He is always right on time.

We were very proud parents at Sha's graduation. Her uncle Bill was also. He decided to let Sha use his restaurant to have a graduation party. She invited her family and friends. Bill's restaurant was right downtown in the heart of the city. Sha, being the Diva that she is, had her uncle post her graduation sign right on top of the building for everyone to see it!

"Mom! Mom!"

"Yes, Sha."

"People are calling saying that they saw my banner on the building."

"So, you feel like a star, don't you? Well, all I can say is enjoy your youth."

"Mom, Uncle Bill said we can stay at the restaurant all night!"

"What? Are you sure?"

"Yep!"

"Okay, Robert will pick you up tomorrow."

We got off the phone, and I just put my feet up on the couch and relaxed. It was Friday, and we had been busy with graduation and then my grandbaby's birthday party. I just wanted to rest. The house was quiet, and Robert was at work. I must have slept at least two hours when the phone started ringing.

"Hello, hello?"

"Hey, this is Cheryl."

"Hi, Cheryl."

I heard a big sigh, then Cheryl paused. Before

she could get a word out, I spoke.

"Cheryl, what's going on?"

"James and Sha have been harassing Chereta."

"What? They are at my brother's in-law's restaurant."

"Yep! They have been calling Chereta's phone threatening her!"

"What? Robert and I don't play that!"

"Neither does Chereta's dad, and he wants to meet with you."

"Hey, Cheryl, let me call you back. I need to call Bill and see what's going on. I thought Chereta was at the restaurant with Sha."

"No, she is at home with me

"Okay, let me call Bill and get to the bottom of what's going on. I will call you back soon."

I hung up with Cheryl and called Bill. The phone rang and rang. As the phone rang, my heart began to race faster and faster. "Lord!" I thought to myself, "Bill, please pick up the phone. Come on Bill! Pick up the phone!"

"Hello?"

"Hey, Bill!"

I could hardly breathe.

"Yeah, Sis?"

"Where is everyone?"

"Oh, they are helping me clean up right now. They had the whole back of the restaurant to themselves. Now, they are cleaning my grills off and sweeping."

"That's good, Bill, but listen."

"What's wrong, Sis?"

Bill sounded puzzled.

"Cheryl called and said that James and Sha have been calling Chereta's phone and threatening her."

"Now sis, that's not true! You know James doesn't have a cell phone. Well, it's broken," chuckled Bill. "That girl has been calling Sha's phone all night! She also called Charles' phone and Cookie's phone. She is mad because she and James broke up, and he's not talking to her! That's what she gets! I will make sure no one calls from here."

"Bill, do that because I don't want any more trouble!! Robert and I don't have time for drama! Let me speak to James!

Hello, James, what's going on?"

"Ma'am?"

"With Chereta?"

"We broke up! The girl keep calling Cookie's and Charles' phone to speak to me! Mom I didn't want to talk to her!"

"Ok listen, I will not have any drama! Don't call her phone!! Tell Cookie and Charles. You know what, let me speak to Cookie!"

"Hi, Mrs. Felicia."

"Hi, Cookie, what's going on?"

"Chereta, oh! Mrs. Felicia, you know I can't stand her. She called my phone for James! I said, 'He don't want to speak to you!' Then, I hung up the phone. Now, you know me Mrs. Felicia, I try to be nice. When she called my phone again after I told her that James didn't want to talk to her, oh, yeah,

I let her have it! Yes, I told her off!" I said, 'Listen, you gold digger, my brother doesn't want you! Now if you call my phone again, I will take CARE OF YOU!!' I'm sorry, Mrs. Felicia! She made me mad!"

"I know, Cookie. She is a gold digger! Look, this girl is dangerous. Just don't answer her calls! Alright?"

"Yes, ma'am."

I got off the phone with Cookie and called Robert.

"Hey, babes!"

"Hey, how are you doing?"

"I'm sorry to call you at work, but we have got a problem!"

"What Chereta?"

"Yep! She said that James and Sha threatened her."

"What? She didn't stay at the restaurant? Oh, that's right. They definitely wouldn't stay the night there together. I don't care if Sha was there."

"Right babe, her mom called me to complain about James and Sha calling Chereta and threatening her. I called Bill, and he said James and Chereta broke up!"

"I don't care if they did break up. I don't want no trouble. That girl is bad news. I'm going to pick them up after I get off work! I will handle this, so don't worry about it."

"But, babe!"

Robert was breathing so hard. It sounded like a tornado wind rushing through the phone.

"What?" Robert sighs.

"Cheryl said she wants to meet with us, along with Chereta's dad."

"Whatever! Okay! We can meet."

"I gotta go. Let me call Bill."

"Okay, I love you."

"Love you too."

Robert doesn't like to be called at work. It gets him off task and messes up his day. I had to call him, so we could work as a team on this one. I knew he would be picking up the kids when he got off work. I believe we had things under control, and we did. At lease on our end, things were under control.

When Sha and James got home, they silently went to their rooms, which was quite alright with Robert and I. That evening, Robert and I ate dinner and talked.

"That girl is not allowed in my house."

"I know that, Robert, I know. James better not even think about letting her in our house."

Robert just looked at me. I know sometimes boys will be boys, but I assured him that Chereta would not step a foot in the house.

We finished dinner and went to bed. We woke up Saturday morning with birds chirping and a sunny, clear sky. It was a good day. On Saturdays, we like to lie in bed and watch T.V. We were watching Robert's favorite show The Best Men, when Cheryl called.

Robert, while looking at the phone, says, "Babes, the phone is ringing."

"Mean!" I yell as I roll over a couple of

pillows to answer the phone. "Hello?"

"Good morning."

"Yes, Cheryl!"

"Chereta wants to speak with Sha."

I rose in bed.

"What?!? Didn't you just call here yesterday complaining about Sha and James threatening Chereta? Didn't you?"

Cheryl answered with a quiet voice; I could hear her ducking her head through the phone.

"Yes, but Chereta needs to talk to Sha."

"Look Cheryl, don't call my house anymore. I don't have any respect for you. You don't call my house, tell me that your daughter is being threatened by my children, and then call and ask for them. I believe you are crazy."

"Uh."

"No, Cheryl, I'm talking."

"Don't call me crazy."

"Cheryl, I'm talking. Something is wrong."

"Chereta just wants her shirt she left at your house."

"No, Cheryl. You come and get it! Make sure you call before you come over!"

"Okay. We don't need to meet. Let's just keep the kids away from each other."

"Cheryl, I believe that won't be a problem."

Time went by and no word from Chereta.

One day, I came home and saw her in my driveway. As soon as I pulled up, she started walking quickly down the driveway and jumped into a white truck. James told me that she brought her work check and wanted him to put it into his account to give her the money for it because her mom wouldn't cash her check.

"Mom, I know we are broken up, but I just want to help her."

"Who's going to help you when your account goes into negative? James just leave that girl alone."

"Yes ma'am."

As James said, "Yes, ma'am", I could see in his eyes that he just wanted to help her. All I cared about was keeping him out of trouble. Robert and I both knew Chereta was trouble. His sisters Mickey and Sha knew it to. Robert and I continued to pray for James and Chereta too. I just prayed that God would open James' eyes and that he would learn a lesson from Chereta. She was a perfect example of a manipulating girl who could one day become a manipulating woman, so I prayed that God would deliver her from that manipulating spirit.

James went on with his life and forgot about Chereta. Robert and I later found out by James and Sha that Chereta had given birth to one child and had one on the way. I thank God for faith and prayer! Without it, our story could have been different, and Chereta could have been in James' life forever as the mother of his children. God answered our prayers. I did not want to be a grandmother and have to worry about the mother of my grandchildren keeping them from us for control reasons.

Faith is not just believing in God for things we can see; it is believing in God no matter what the situation appears to be. I hope that as you finish this chapter of faith, you will begin to make your own declarations of faith for your family. I will add to the back of the book to help you start a faith declaration journal.

CHAPTER 16

GOD CALLS US TO HAVE ORDER

God calls us to order because He loves and adores us. He wants us to receive the gifts and blessing that He has for us. He calls us to order to perform His work throughout the earth that His name will be made great.

He wants us to be His servants here on earth. I have chosen to serve others through sharing my experiences with you including the good, the bad, and the ugly. Only Christ can take someone like me and use me to help others. My mother was fifteen when she had me, and my father was twenty-one. My grandmother Coleen (Cora) Billups gave my mom to the Lord and literally lifted me up with her arms stretched towards heaven saying, "Lord, use this one for your glory."

Every morning when she would wake up, she would yell, "Thank you Jesus!" and grab the olive oil to anoint my head. I was marked with the seal of the cross and bathed in righteousness. From that day, I began to walk out the plan that God had for my life.

As I got older, the enemy tried to destroy me on many occasions. I would preach to students on the playground at recess. One day, I preached to a man driving the lunch truck. He went to the office to tell the principal. The principal, Mr. Willis, threatened to paddle me if I didn't stop preaching.

In my early twenties, I was in and out of church. While hanging out with my friends and going to clubs, I was still preaching. I made wrong choices and turned away from my upbringing at times. Still, God had His hands on me. I can still hear some of the words my grandmother used to pray for me, her and my Aunt Mary. I can hear them saying, "Lord, this one. Lord, this is your child." Through all my mishaps and wrong doings, grace and mercy followed me.

"Order my steps in thy word: and let not any iniquity have dominion over me" (Psalms 119:113, KJV).

Thank God, I haven't been consumed by iniquity! I'm walking out God's plan for my life daily. The Word of God orders my steps. The more I read His word, the more it comes alive in my heart. I believe that the words we speak over our lives and the lives of our children are powerful. These words help to lead us down the path that we need to go down. Our words can lead us down the right road or wrong road. We need to align our words with the Word of God.

"Let the words of my mouth and the meditation of my heart, be acceptable in thy sight, O Lord, my strength, and my redeemer" (Psalm 19:14, KJV).

"Let no corrupt communication proceed out of your mouth, but that which is good to the use of edifying, that it may minister grace unto the hearers" (Ephesians 4:29, KJV).

Thank God for a praying grandmother, mother, and aunt. Now, I can live out the promises of God by what they have declared over my life. I can also speak life into any situation I'm in.

I heard that God had a plan for my life at an early age. I accepted Christ as my Lord and Savior at the age of ten. I believe I was a lot younger than ten years old, but I was ten when I received the Holy Spirit. God calls us to have order in our lives when we choose to follow Him. He doesn't make us have order in our lives. We must answer His call. The Bible says that a good man's steps are ordered by Him.

"The steps of a good man are ordered by the Lord: and he delighted in his way" (Psalm 37:23, KJV).

When we accept His leadership, we become righteous by following His plan, which guides our steps. Isn't it nice to have a tour guide when we go on tours? It takes so much longer wandering around and trying to find places with no maps or tour guides. Without a guide, it can turn what should be a nice tour into a disaster. With a leader, we can just follow along and enjoy the serenity.

I know families that have no guidance and no map to follow. What good is a map if it's not open and no one's following the directions on it? What good is the Bible to us if we don't follow the instructions on the page? The Bible teaches us that when we think, our way is right, it's not. Our flesh never wants what's good for us.

"There is a way which seemeth right unto a man, but the end thereof are the ways of death" (Psalm 14:12).

The only way we can train our flesh to do what is right is by the Word. We need to have the mind of Christ.

"Let this mind be in you, which was also in

Christ Jesus" (Philippians 2:5, KJV).

People tend to argue that the Bible doesn't give instructions for the family. I have given you several scriptures in this book alone. I urge you to answer God's call, then you will understand His instructions. You'll have peace in your life and hope for your family. Your life will never be the same!

CHAPTER 17

CLEANSING

We all need to be cleansed at some point in our lives. No one is perfect or always right. None of us were perfect as children, and we are sure not perfect as adults. I certainly wasn't the best child, but I came close to it! Not by a long shot. I was a typical kid of the seventies, stubborn.

Sometimes, we get residue on us from others that might leave our lives a mess. At times, it might cause us not to even know who we are. If we don't know who we are, anyone can say things about us and our families. Christ builds us up in the areas where we have allowed people to tear us down. It is imperative that we receive a cleansing from God to rid us of all pass hurts, especially pain from our families. We don't want to carry that residue into our families.

When we design our family after the Word of God, we need to understand that ministry starts at home. Therefore, we must cleanse each other, our mate, and our children. My husband had to clean me from the single-mother syndrome. My conversation always had to do with me being a single parent, until one day when he got tired of it. He said, "Look babe, you have not been a single mother for a while now!"

I thought about it, and I replied softly, "You're right!"

I began to search my heart, "Why am I doing this?"

I was married but still living as a single mom in some ways. If something was wrong, I had to fix it because that's what I was used to doing. I always had plan A, B, and C. I'm sure a lot of single parents can relate to that. I was married but stuck in past routines. I didn't realize that I needed to be cleansed, and that cleansing would come from my husband. He cleansed me by letting me know that we're in this together. I have a shoulder, not just to lean on but his shoulders are also strong enough to hold me up so I won't fall. My speech had to be cleansed.

I had to realize that we both are parents.

These children are not my children. They are God's children given to us as a gift. To our children, we are their parents. They may have a biological father, but we are their parents. We are nourishing them through the Word of God!

We as parents will also have to offer cleansing to our children from time to time. Cleansing of the mind seems to be the one we offer the most. Children are taught so many things by teachers, their peers, and the communities that they're raised in.

We really do a disservice to our boys and young men, by teaching them to suppress their feelings. Boys are told not to cry when they're younger. If they fall or scrape their knees, some will yell at them to "Suck it up!" Men are made to be able to bear a lot of weight, but sometimes the weight may be more than what he can bear on his own. We know that we can transfer this weight to Christ, and He will bear it.

How do we help our young men and boys?

Maybe their weights are high expectations and doing everything on their own. I remember having a conversation with my son, James, about asking for help. He said that he didn't know if he would get help if he asked, because he is a young man and should be independent. My heart sank, James is the second oldest of four children. He's also the only boy, so he was raised to have tough skin. I did teach him to be strong and independent. It was never my intention to give him the impression that he had to do everything on his own. I just wanted him to grow up to be a man that loved Christ and would provide for his family. I started the cleansing process with him by letting him know that if he needed something, Robert and I would always be there for him. If we can help him, we will. I began to tear down the walls, he was surrounded by.

"Son, you have a job. You're paying bills; you paid off your own car. That's all I want is for you to be a responsible young man. We all need help sometimes."

"Thanks, mom," he replied with a smile saying, "Mom, do you have twenty dollars I can borrow until Friday?"

"Yes, go and get my purse." I gave him my bank card and off he went.

Perhaps he had been struggling for some time with inner thoughts such as, "You're a young man. You must find your own way. You don't need to ask anyone for anything, not even your parents."

Purifying the mind with new thoughts is the beginning of the cleansing of our minds. Taking on the mind of Christ is the next step, so we must reject negative thoughts and start living a positive life.

We teach our boys not to cry, and we want our men to be strong. We need to teach our boys to cry out to Jesus. We need to let our men know that we understand that they must be weak enough to accept Christ.

I mentioned in previous chapters that women

are the weaker vessels, and if women are weaker, someone must be weak. This means that the men must have a need for God's help. Men are strong in the natural sense but weak in a spiritual sense. We are teaching them right by not allowing them to give up easy and knowing that all help comes from God. Without him, we're nothing. If you fall, get back up.

We also don't want them to be too strong to express their feelings. This includes worship. Men need to experience a true worship experience with Christ. Not only do they need to experience a true worship experience, but they also need to know how to show love, hurt, and anger in a proper way.

As women, we may be emotional. It's easy for most of us to cry and express our feelings of hurt, love, and anger. What about our girls and young women? I'm sure they need cleansing too. How about a cleansing of their minds? I'm sure someone has told them somewhere not to depend on a man for anything. The Bible even speaks of man failing.

I understand why a lot of girls and women

won't take a man's word at face value. They're waiting for him to slip and mess up. As parents raising them after the heart of God, we have to change their minds. We cleanse them through their father's good examples, knowing that they should mean what they say and keep their promises. If they can't keep their word, there should be an explanation as to why they didn't keep their word. This will change their minds and set them free of some of the trust issues. Help them choose husbands they can trust and hold accountable. I know some of this might not be easy for fathers to do. Being the head of the household, he may feel like he doesn't have to explain himself to anyone. Right? Wrong!

We will all answer to Christ on judgment day. I don't think men who are fathers and husbands want to have to answer to God as to why they never kept their word to their family. What would their report look like? They will answer to creating mistrust in their wives and children. If you are a father, I beg you. Please don't let this be you! Fathers, if you are reading this book and you see yourself as creating mistrust in your love one's life, let the cleansing start now for you and your love ones.

First, just admit to failing to keep your word, and then apologize to your love ones. Ask God to help you keep your word. When you can't keep your word, be accountable and explain why.

"If we confess our sins, he is faithful and just to forgive us [our] sins, and to cleanse us from all unrighteousness" (1 John 1:9).

God knows we are not perfect. We all make mistakes. The Lord just wants us to admit our shortcomings and ask for His help.

"And be not conformed to this world: but be ye transformed by the renewing of your mind that ye may prove what [is] that good, and acceptable, and perfect, will of God" (Romans 12:2).

I like this scripture about transforming and renewing the mind. When girls see that they have fathers who are committed to their well-being and accountable for their actions, they will be able to know what is good, acceptable, and perfect for them in the will of God. Awesome! No one will be able to paint it in their minds that there are no good men left in the world!

"Having therefore these promises, dearly beloved, let us cleanse ourselves from all filthiness of the flesh and spirit, perfecting holiness in the fear of God" (2 Corinthians 7:1).

The dictionary's meaning of cleanse is "To free from dirt, defilement, or guilt; purge or clean". When we're cleansing our family, let's make sure we are freeing them from any dirt, defilement, or guilt. Leave no room for the enemy to invade. Let's purify each other clean through the Word of God!

I spoke a lot about cleansing of the mind. We do need our mind, body, and soul cleansed. I'm no expert. I do believe if our minds are clear from file thoughts, it won't lead our body to do negative things. Then our souls will have nowhere to roam; they will belong to Christ. The Bible says let this mind be in you which was also in Christ Jesus.

CHAPTR 18

A HOUSE OF PEACE

True peace only comes from God. Order in the House gives you some basic principles for the family with a foundation built on God. In the previous chapters, you were giving many tools to use to set order in your family. Practicing these things won't bring you peace in your home. Let just say sometimes your family won't appear to be peaceful. There will be some resistance to following God's way instead of your own way. I want you to know that if you haven't allowed Christ to be the C.E.O. of your family but you have decided to now, it will get easier.

The more you get to know Him through His word, the more you will love Him. You will begin to have a sense of God's plan for your family. Those things you used to practice that didn't mean you any good, will fall off.

Surround yourself with good families in

Christ, good families' period. Remember everyone may not do the same things in their households the way that you may do them. Just make sure they have the same C.E.O. as you. Make sure they are following His orders, as you are.

If you are a single parent, surround yourself with other single parents who are displaying the values of Christ. True peace comes when we surrender our will to Christ and follow Him in everything that we do.

Peace is resting in Him no matter what your circumstances may be. Knowing and believing that he indeed has you. He will provide for you. You can take that to the bank. When He has full authority in our lives, He will go beyond that which we could ask or think.

"Now to him who is able to do immeasurably more than all we ask or imagine, according to his power that is at work within us" (Ephesians 3:20, NIV).

"But my God shall supply all your need according to his riches in glory by Christ Jesus" (Philippians 4:1, KJV).

Not too long after Robert and I got married, I hurt my back. I don't know if it happened at work or if it came from the scoliosis that I had been diagnosed with. We got married in October 2006; we both had full time jobs and a lot on our plate. As a newly married couple, there was so much that we were planning to do. Being off work due to my back pain wasn't in the plan at all. Robert and I have a lot of goals now, but we had even more in 2006.

One day, I went to Wendy's for lunch with a group of my co-workers. We were all in the car laughing and talking. I noticed that the talking had stop. We had pulled into Wendy's. All I could hear was the car door slamming. My co-workers were either hungry or happy to be away from the work place. I went to get out of the car, and I couldn't move. The muscles in my back had stiffened up just that quickly from sitting in the car for less than ten minutes. I couldn't get out of the car. My friend Tina noticed,

"Hey, Felicia. You coming? What's wrong?"

Trying to hold back the tears in my eyes from the pain, I yelled out, "No, I don't want anything."

Everyone got their food and got back in the car. They laughed and picked up their conversation right where they left off.

"Felicia. Why aren't you eating?"

I remained quiet, while my friend Tina just changed the subject.

When we got back to work, my back was stiff; I could barely move. I was working two jobs, one as a machine operator and one as an outreach worker in healthcare. On this day, I was working on the machine on a ten-hour shift. Standing wasn't in my favor. I would bend down to put mail on the machine only to rise up in pain. I had to do something!

After going to work and not being able to get out of the car to go into Wendy's for lunch, I went to the doctor's office. They took x-rays and said that I had lower lumbar pain. I went to the chiropractor's

office to relieve the pain. I would call them from work crying in pain. They would squeeze me in without an appointment. When started

missing a lot of work, my supervisor suggested that maybe I should go on medical leave. I went on a medical leave and later was considered as retired.

Our income was cut in half. There wasn't a day where we went without food or anything that we needed. We still had peace with very little income. Peace doesn't come from our surroundings or our circumstances. We may have peace in our surroundings and circumstances, but that's not peace itself. People will gather themselves around a lot of people who are happy and successful, yet still be in turmoil. You may see a smile on their faces, yet there's no peace within.

Some people say that water is soothing and relaxing. I love water; I love to watch the fish of all types. I really love big bright fish. Most of all I love to hear the ocean, the waves rushing through the water. There's nothing like hearing the water hit the rocks. For me, this is relaxing; and this environment is peaceful.

I would love to live in a peaceful world without violence and hate. A world full of love would be considered peaceful to me. We all know that's not the case in this world. To have peace in this world, we need faith and assurance that there's something more than this life. A relationship with our Creator who has promised us an afterlife if we accept Him, Jesus Christ as our Lord and Savior, gives us something more. That's peace; it's an eternal peace. It will never go away no matter what my circumstances are.

Poor or rich, it doesn't matter. Time and time again, I have seen people who are successful, where money is not an issue for them. Yet, they still aren't happy. Most of them don't even have a clue as to why they are so unhappy. True peace will bring the happiness they are longing for. Where there's a lack of peace, there's no fulfillment in this life.

Many believe that having a family brings happiness. Some will have families only to discover they're still not happy. Happiness is short-lived without peace. Without peace, the happiness that we seek in money will vanish. Having peace from God will allow us to enjoy the fruits of our labor. We go through so many different things in this life; our circumstances can change overnight. Nothing is for sure in this life, but a beginning and ending. If you exist, you had a beginning, and you will have an ending.

I'm glad I have a life with Christ, so after this life, I will have eternal life. My relationship with Christ brings me peace, and it's because of that peace that I can enjoy true happiness. I'm content with things and without things. I'm happy through my storms in life. "When there's no sunshine, I rely on God's solar power" (Quote from my second book, Think on These Things: A Word for you Today). We can have peace in this life, peace in our homes, and peace with our families.

CHAPTER 19

NO MORE SHAME

There were many unmarried parents when I was younger. There are still a lot of unmarried parents today. Some things we just can't change. I was a single parent, but I don't bear the shame from being a single parent. I am now married and have been for about nine years. There's a lot more benefits and blessing from having children through marriage. All parents will go through trials and blessings.

After we have been cleansed and delivered, we need to move on. Start over new. God will give you a fresh start. Maybe you weren't a single parent, but you drank and used drugs around your children. It doesn't matter if you did drugs or were an alcoholic. You can't go back to those days and erase the past. Don't allow your children to bring up your past. Live your life for today. Be the best parent to your children now. If they are grown, pray that God will open up their hearts. If they are young, pray that they won't be too damaged by your bad choices.

Guilt will keep you stuck in one place and in the very minute where you made the bad choice. Families should help repair and restore each other. My dad is an alcoholic. He has had a problem with alcohol since I was young. The enemy has him so ashamed that he just keeps drinking. As for me, I love my dad dearly. When I look at him, I see my dad, not a drunk. When I would go visit him, I would treat him like he was the best parent in the world. I would let him know how much I needed him, that I loved him and forgave him a long time ago. I prayed that he would allow God to release him from shame, so he can live the life God wants him to live.

If you are a child who is carrying shame around, let it go. You need to be who God has intended for you to be. You can't go back to the days where you treated your parents so cruel. Maybe you are shameful because your eyes are now open and you realize what you did was wrong. You wish you could let your parents know how sorry you are, but they've already passed away. You can be delivered and cleansed, but if shame remains, you will still be bound. It's okay to be sorry, not shameful. People who are living in shame run and hide. They feel like everyone knows what a bad child or parent they were or are. Maybe people do know. As I said before, you can't change the past, but you can start changing your ways now. People who spend so much time focusing on your errors and mistakes can't possibly be working on their own errors and mistakes. Believe me, we all have sinned.

"For all have sinned and fall short of the glory of God" (Romans 3:23, NIV).

Shame can and will cripple you by not allowing you to be the best that you can be in the moment when you're needed. Grown children still need their parents to be present and active in their lives. Don't you believe for one second that they are grown and they don't need you. Adults still need someone to lean on for advice, or even a shoulder to cry on.

When I became a "Meme" (grandma), I needed my parents more than ever. I have always been told that I am such a good parent. Grandma at thirty-eight! No way! I couldn't believe it. I wondered what kind of grandmother I would be.

Robert and I were always on the go. We are still young ourselves. When our first grandchild was born, I asked my mom a lot of questions. After all, I had made her a grandmother at a young age also. I often wondered how she felt about being a young grandmother. Talking to her, I found out that she shared some of the same feelings that I had. We all need our parents in some way or another. There are so many situations where guilt can overtake us and bury us in our own shame. There should be no place for shame in our families. We need to build each other up.

CHAPTER 20

HONORING OUR FAMILY MEMBERS

Honoring our family members is necessary. Since principles start at home, we need to show each other how to honor others. When we see our children displaying the values we have taught them, we need to acknowledge it by letting them know how proud we are of them. It's hard sometimes to stand for what's right when others are doing wrong. Our young people are smart. They have a lot to offer our world. They need encouragement to make good decisions.

Our youngest daughter is in high school in the tenth grade. Her friends have been dating, so she came to me and asked if she could go on a date. My heart started beating fast. I took a deep breath and asked, "With who?"

She began to tell me that there was a boy named Joshua who wanted her to go to movies with him.

"Do you like Joshua? What do you like so

much about Joshua? Is he a Christian?"

"Yes Mom."

"How do you know that?"

"Well, he goes to church."

"Yes, but is he living a Christian life?"

"I think he is."

"I don't think you should be dating right now. I do believe you should have positive relationships with the opposite sex. You are too young to have a boyfriend. If you like him, you are only allowed to go to the movies with a group. We must know who your friends are that you are spending time with. I want you to know you are young, and you will be interested in boys. That's natural, but we will set guidelines for you to follow. We do not want you to be alone with a boy under any circumstances. Not because we don't trust you, but because we love you. Robert and I just don't want you to be in a situation to where you are compromising your moral values for feelings and emotions. We know more and more young people are having sex at your age. That's not going to be you; you will know what to do with your emotions and feelings when you like a boy."

"Mom, I know I have to go places in a group, but why can't I have a boyfriend? I'm almost sixteen. You said I can date at age sixteen."

"Yes, as long as you know how to use the tools that we have given you to keep yourself until marriage. We encourage you to enjoy your youth. We do not want you to be worried about boys so much to where you are distracted."

I was so glad our daughter Tina came to me and asked me could she date.

Later on that evening, I shared the conversation that Tina and I had with Robert. Well, it didn't go too well. I said,

"Sweet, Tina and I had an interesting conversation today about dating."

"There will be no dating here! Who is it?"

"His name is-"

"I don't care what his name is, because there will be no dating."

"Sweet, please listen to me. Please. I told her she could have a friend."

"Yeah right, a friend that's a boyfriend."

"No Poppy, she's not sixteen. We need her to continue to be honest with us. A lot of young people aren't so honest with their parents. They are making decisions without them."

"That's true, and I hear what you're saying, but I just don't want her dating anyone. Just bring me the boy!"

"I know dear, but we just need to be smart about how we deal with this situation."

After Robert and I had the very intense conversation, we slept on it. We prayed about it and decided that we will let her have friends of the opposite sex that she can go places with in a group. When she's old enough, we won't have to go over dating rules again because she already knows them.

Robert and I met Josh. Needless to say, their friendship didn't last that long. One day, I asked Tina if she had talked to Josh, and she said she was not talking to Joshua anymore. I asked her why, and she said that Joshua wanted to have sex with her. My heart started to beat fast, but I had to stay calm. I asked her what she said to him. She said that she told him she wasn't going to have sex with him, so he told her their friendship was over. I felt bad. Tina was heartbroken, but I told her how proud we were of her and how a lot of young people don't make the right decision under pressure, which is hard when you like someone. Joshua may go and find another girl and have sex with her, which is sad because he's only fifteen-years-old. At the rate he's going, he will be a teen parent.

When we honor each other in our home, we are compelled to honor others. We honored Tina for standing up for what is right. When we honor each other, we help build one another up.

Imagine having a family without any honor. What would that family look like? I think you would see a lot of ungrateful people, who just take people for granted. With thoughts like, "You're my children and you're supposed to do well", "There's no need to say, 'thank you'", and "Oh, you're doing well in school, you're supposed to, what do you want a prize?" there's no expression of gratitude.

What would it be like for our spouses? Maybe we would accept their gifts without a "thank you" because after all, they love us and they are supposed to make us happy. Why not celebrate each other? We made a vow to each other "Until death do we part". I'm sure you get the picture. Everyone wants to be appreciated. When we learn this, our families will demonstrate to others how to show love and appreciation. I find myself going out of my way to point out the good in others. When I receive good service at a restaurant, I leave a good tip and I let the manager know how pleased I was with the service that I received. It's so easy to find negative things to say about others. We need to look for ways to honor each other. It's my prayer that you make it your goal, as I have, to make others smile by how we show them our appreciation.

CHAPTER 21

STICKING IT OUT

Sometimes it's hard to stick with the rules you have set for your home. Some are Biblical, and some may be things that you have set for your home that are not outright outlined in the Bible, like "no sagging". We have one son. He has grown up to be an honorable young man. It wasn't hard for me to tell him not to sag at all. That wasn't the image that I wanted him to portray. When he got to high school, most boys were sagging their pants. James would say he wasn't sagging. I would catch him at times sagging, so I would stay on him. Then, he started to pull his shirt way down over his pants. For the most part, he wasn't sagging.

Now with the girls, I had to stick it out on many issues. One was not spending the night over at their friends' houses. They weren't allowed to spend the night at many people's houses. In fact, they were only allowed to spend the night over at a few friends' houses. I had to meet their parents and try to get to know their beliefs and who else lived in their household. My oldest daughter would get upset when I asked too many questions. She had one friend who I went through my usual questions and whole routine with, only to find out that her household was not somewhere that I wanted my daughter to be. I picked her friend up to take them to the mall, she had a short mini skirt on. I said "Oh no, you better tell her before I do. She will not be going nowhere with us with that short skirt on. Oh, no!" My daughter had a talk with the girl, and yes indeed, she changed her skirt.

When I dropped her off to her house, I got the surprise of my life. I saw a person come running out of her house towards my car. I couldn't tell if she was a woman or a girl. She had on the same skirt as my daughter's friend, May. Wow, this was her mom. I rolled down my window.

"Hey, Girley."

I just kept looking her up and down. She didn't even notice, she just kept on talking.

"Girl we've got to go hang out."

I looked out the corner of my eye; I couldn't

believe my eyes! I blinked once and then again. I saw a man holding a 40-ounce bottle of beer; he wobbled and went to sit on her porch.

"What?!?" I thought to myself and looked at my daughter. Ms. Rollins, May's mom, waved at me "See ya, girl."

I nodded. Then, she walked down the street. Now it was just dusk. My mind began to run wild. "My God, my God, where is this woman going? Where could she be going with that hot skirt on leaving her girls home with that man? Yes, the one sitting on the porch with the 40-ounce.

I shouted to May, "May, hey do you want to come back to my house? Will you be okay?"

May lowered her head and snickered to herself, "Yes I'm okay."

"Really?" I looked at my daughter. She turned her head.

"Really, mom. Yes, ma'am."

"Ok."

I drive off. I begin to pray. "God, please protect May. Now, I know that's her mom's boyfriend, friend, but I don't trust him. I need you to put a hedge around her, Lord."

Then, I turned and looked at my daughter. "Oh, you will never go back over to that house. Do you hear me? NEVER!"

My daughter Mickey began to speak; I stopped her as I put my hand up. "No, I said, 'NEVER!' Now, I like May. She can come over here, but you will never go over there again."

I had three children by myself for a while, two girls and one son. Many of the times I needed a break and help, I went through a lot of pressure as a single parent. It was never okay for me to leave my children with anyone. I explained this to my daughter. I wish that there were more parents who I could trust to care for my children. Then, they could have spent the night over at their friends' houses like other children. All parents are not raising their children under the authority of God. I told Mickey,

"You were raised by the principles of God. Being around other teenagers doesn't give you a right to act the same way that they do."

I wanted to snatch May's mom and smack her. It's better to kill people with kindness and love than vengeance and hate. Live by example, so they can see Christ in our lives. When I change my way of thinking to deal with things in a positive way, often times it changes the outcome of the situation. We must stick it out for our children by standing firm.

If you are married, then you already know that marriage is choosing to stick it out. Some people say marriage is work, but unless you're together, there's nothing to work on. In marriage, we will go through different phases, just as we do in life in general. You have the dating stage where everything is lovely and fun. The engagement is fun also, but it can also be stressful. Planning a wedding can be bittersweet. I've even heard of people almost losing friendships over planning a wedding. There are some "bridezillas" out there. I guess? I wasn't one.

After being engaged, there's the wedding

which can also be stressful. The wedding day is full of bliss and love, unless you're one of the couples who argue on the wedding day. After the "I do's", there's the honeymoon stage.

Robert and I would stay in bed all day on the weekend, watch movies, eat, and just look at each other. I was so happy to be married that I always referred to Robert as my husband. I hardly ever used his name. I would wake up in the morning and just look at him. I just couldn't believe that we were married.

I didn't even want to go places with other couples, not even with my best friend Evelyn and her husband Jim. Evelyn was surprised at first, because we are so close. We had been planning our lives since we were about ten-years-old. I think since Robert and I had been friends for ten years before we got married, I just wanted him all to myself. It seems that our honeymoon stage lasted forever.

We have been married for eight and a half years now. I've just started to do some things without Robert. Two to three years after being married, we were settled and relaxed with each other. We knew the good, the bad, and the ugly about each other, as far as living together; and we were ok with it. In the settling-in stage, outside people, who mean well, start asking questions like are going to have kids, or buy a house? We weren't in a rush to buy a house; we wanted to establish how we paid our bills and managed our finances first.

Now having children was a different story being that I had four and Robert didn't have any of his own. We had already discussed maybe having two. Since we had been friends long before we got married, he already knew how I felt about having more children. I was open to having at least one more child. I had our last daughter at the age of twenty-eight. I say our last daughter because Robert considers all of the children his. We went from wanting to have two children, to one, and to none together. We still ended up with four. Our family planning just didn't work out to where we had children together. Not because we couldn't, but because we were too into each other and raising the children that we already had. Robert told me to leave well enough alone. I pushed and pushed because of what people said. Then, Robert strongly told me to leave it alone.

We are good people, and we love children so much. I do wonder from time to time what our little one would look like, or be like. Robert and I love our life the way it is, and we wouldn't change a thing.

I have learned that during the settling-in stage of marriage is when people look to see what the new couple is doing. Buying a house or having children are at the top of the list, when people are looking for growth. Some people are just plain, ole nosey; they just want to know the 411, your business.

I share our story with you to tell you that whatever stage you're in during your marriage, hang in there. Robert and I have a lot of support from our family; Both of our families are strong. If people would say, "Wow, she has four children", my mother-in-law would be quick to shut them down. She'd say, "And? My husband Patrick had seven children when we got married. We had two, and we have nine altogether."

Yes, they were all their children, before and after marriage, just like Robert and I. Can't nobody put a family together like God!

I never really gave it a thought that I wouldn't get married because I had four children. I was raised to wait until marriage, as many people from my generation, but I didn't. I always had a heart for God, yet I did as many people from the seventies did, I found things out own my own. I was in long-term relationships from the age of eighteen. My grandmother always taught me that children are a blessing from God, no matter how they come. She also said when we are in sin or make an error in our lives; we must go before the Lord for forgiveness. My heart was right; I had asked God for forgiveness for having children out of wedlock a long time ago. I just asked Him to forgive me for not waiting on Him period.

I never believed that I would be married with four children, and I thank God that he gave me the mother in-law that I have. She always says, "You're a blessing to Robert, and I thank you for giving him a family."

I'm tearful just writing this, because God is so awesome. We talked about the dating, the engagement, the honeymoon, and the settling-in stage. What about the comfortable stage? This is the stage where a couple has been married about ten years. They are so comfortable to where they feel like neither of them are going anywhere. They find themselves gaining weight and letting themselves go. They don't like trying new things, or even being motivated to go anywhere. They are comfortable where they are at work and at home. This is a very dangerous stage in marriage!

In this stage, we need to stick it out! Hang in there, and fall in love all over again. I'm sure this will take us through the next ten years to get to twenty. Bringing back passion that has been lying dormant is not easy. It can be done through time with dedication and patience. I share these stories briefly as a foundation for the family.

This will be addressed more in volume two of Order in the House. Your family will have dry seasons with your children as well as in your marriage. Stay firm. Weather the storm and recreate a new passion for one another.

CHAPTER 22

USE YOUR RESOURCES

Asking for help doesn't mean that we have failed; it means that we acknowledge that we don't have the answers. When we are in an unfamiliar area in our lives and when we face things we have never been faced with before, why struggle through it if you don't have to?

I can remember when the children were young; I was in a program called "I Care". It was for families who needed support with their children. We met up at least twice a week. They had activities for the children and adults; this group supported the family as a whole. Each family was provided with resources to help them with their day-to-day needs. The people in this group became my friends.

At the time, I had a five-year-old, three-year-old, and a two-year-old. The two-year-old and the three-year-old were only ten months apart. I felt like I had twins. I was in my early twenties with three kids. I had lots of crisis, from losing jobs because of scheduling or missing work due to one of the children being sick. I needed encouragement and guidance. This program helped me live a life with structure. I sought help as a single mom. It's better to get help than go through life with blinders on.

There is help out there for your family, single family or married, whatever your status as a family may be. Unfortunately, people won't always volunteer to help you. Don't blame them; they don't know your needs. Keep searching for whatever your needs are for your family. Go to your church community, friends, and extended family. Do your research. Find out what resources there are for families. If you are a single mother or father, get with other single parents and support each other.

Being a parent is a joy, but it can be stressful. Having three children in my early twenties, I couldn't afford many activities; but I managed to use what I had. I would pack sandwiches with snacks for the kids in the summer. Off to the beach, we would go. We would go in the afternoon and leave at night. The beach was a fun activity without spending a lot of money. The children enjoyed themselves just the same.

CHAPTER 23

PRAYER

Knowing how to pray is the best tool you can have for your family. Prayer is essential for the family. Prayer activates our faith, believing and expecting great thing from God. We must learn how to pray for our own families, instead of always asking others to pray for us. We should be inviting them to pray with us. It's good to have others join us in prayer.

"Where two or three are gathered together in my name, there am I in the midst of them" (Matthew 18:20-22, KJV).

This verse is a statement of promise; He will be in the midst of our prayer when we come together in His name. The key is praying in His name. If we gather in His name, He will be with us. If we pray in His name, He is in our midst.

Being in our midst doesn't mean that He will answer every prayer the way we want Him to. He will come in between our natural ram and spiritual ram and seek out our needs and wants according to His Word. Number one, God doesn't answer prayers that are contrary to His Word. Through studying the Word of God, we will learn the right way to pray.

His Word says that He will give us the desire of our hearts in Psalms 37:4-11. Read this scripture in your spare time. It also speaks of trusting in God, and He will bring things to pass.

This is great, that scripture tells me that if I line my heart up with the things that are pleasing to God, He will answer my prayers according to His Word. Now if your prayer is for your family to be men, then of course, your heart is not right. If your desire is for your family to be blessed so that others acknowledge God through His Work in your life, then your intent for the blessings of God on your family is good. Most of the time we know our intent on the things we want from God, and so does He. Sometimes we might have the spirit of greed and not be aware of it. God reveals all things through the Holy Spirit. His answer to our prayer may be silent, because He's waiting for us to get to the place where He can bless us. The choice is ours to live our life according to His Word. God won't make us do anything. If we have given Christ the authority over our lives, He will not let people, places, or things rule us.

Many times, we get so mad when things don't go our way. The next time you get mad or wonder why God hasn't answered your prayers, ask yourself who has authority over your life. If it is God, then trust Him to do what is best for you and your family. He has promise in His Word not to withhold any good thing from us. He will not give us the good thing, whatever it is, if our hearts are not right. He will not allow things or possessions to destroy us, nor will he allow us to self-destruct by being vain.

That's when we have made Him the C.E.O. of our lives. If He doesn't have the authority over your life, He is not in control over your life. You have not invited Him into your life. To accept Him is a choice. We seem to want to make decisions without God, then pray for Him to fix things. When he doesn't fix things the way we want Him to, we get mad at Him. We must know that God loves us so much; He is just waiting for us to obey by His Word so, He can bless us. He has blessed us even when we don't deserve it because of His love and mercy.

I saved this chapter for last; I want you to know there is power in prayer. Praying the right way is the key to unlocking God's blessings over our lives, we get to know Him through his word and our prayers. I pray that you get to know Christ if you don't know Him. Today is the day to start getting to know Him.

Trust Him with your family. His Word is true, and it's a firm foundation for the family. I pray this book will be a reference book for your family. From this day forth, you will allow God to be the Chief Executive Officer in your home.

ORDER IN THE HOUSE:

STUDY: SCRIPTURES & NOTES

What are the areas that I haven't allowed God to lead me in?

_____

_____

_____

_____

_____

_____

_____

_____

_____

_____

ORDER IN THE HOUSE:

Why?

_____

_____

_____

_____

_____

The Ten Commandments

1.

2.

3.

4.

5.

6.

7.

8.

9.

ORDER IN THE HOUSE:

10.

Write down the commandment that you're having the most trouble with.

_____

_____

_____

_____

_____

_____

Write down why this commandment is hard for you.

_____

_____

_____

_____

_____

STUDY: "THE BEATITUDES"

The Bible doesn't call these scriptures "The Beatitudes". Biblical scholars named these scriptures because each scripture is a blessing. This is the "Sermon on the Mount of Olives".

Introduction to the Sermon on the Mount

"Now when Jesus saw the crowds, he went up on a mountainside and sat down. His disciples came to him, and he began to teach them" (Matthew 5:1-2, NIV).

The Beatitudes

3"Blessed are the poor in spirit,
for theirs is the kingdom of heaven
4Blessed are those who mourn,
for they will be comforted.
5Blessed are the meek,
for they will inherit the earth
6Blessed are those who hunger and thirst for righteousness,
for they will be filled.
7Blessed are the merciful,

for they will be shown mercy
8Blessed are the pure in heart,
for they will see God,
9Blessed are the peacemakers,
for they will be called children of God.
10Blessed are those who are persecuted because of righteousness, for theirs is the kingdom of heaven.
11Blessed are you when people insult you, persecute you and falsely say all kinds of evil against you because of me. 12 Rejoice and be glad, because great is your reward in heaven, for in the same way they persecuted the prophets who were before you"
(Matthew 5:3-12, NIV).

PRAYERS FOR YOUR FAMILY

Start with The Lord's Prayer. Write it down.
Matthew 6:9-13

The Prayer of Jabez (Chronicles 4:10)

ORDER IN THE HOUSE:

Write down what you feel about forgiveness.

Look up scriptures in the Bible on forgiveness. Tip: you can Google it by searching "forgiveness Bible". You will then get a list of scriptures from the KJV, NIV, and other versions. Write down as many scriptures as you can. Recite them with your family.

ORDER IN THE HOUSE:

FELICE

Write down what love means to you.

Write down as many scriptures as you can find on love.

ORDER IN THE HOUSE:

Recite them. Practice it in your home. Speak good words to your family, your husband (or wife) and children.

Husband (or wife), I love you because_____

_____

_____

_____

_____

_____

_____

Children_____

_____

_____

_____

_____

Write down why God loves you.

ORDER IN THE HOUSE:

Write down what His love means to you.

ORDER IN THE HOUSE:

Write down what you want God to do for your family.

ORDER IN THE HOUSE:

Find scriptures on faith write them down

_____
_____
_____
_____
_____
_____
_____
_____
_____

Ways to honor your family.

_____
_____
_____
_____
_____

ORDER IN THE HOUSE:

STAY CONNECTED

Like my Facebook page: Felice

Follow on Twitter: @Author Felice

Always go to Google for more book information.

Go to Barnes and Noble stores and check for books. They can order them to the store.

Future authors, please visit my website:

www.rightsidepublishing.com

For booking events, please e-mail me at

felice@rightsidepublishing.com

ORDER IN THE HOUSE:

AUTHOR FELICE
AND HUSBAND ROBERT

ORDER IN THE HOUSE:

www.ingramcontent.com/pod-product-compliance
Lightning Source LLC
Chambersburg PA
CBHW071157300426
44113CB00009B/1236